MW01204888

"Witho youth ministry books I've ever read! I've been in youth ministry for 40 years and I'm still "junior" compared to the years, experience, knowledge, and wisdom of Bob Johns. He is a legend in the space of youth ministry but he didn't write this book from an ivory tower, rather he wrote it as a sage, in the trenches of the local church, who knows how important it is to help other youth workers. His stories are fun and inspiring and his ideas are practical and helpful (from "respect the janitor" to "pursuing excellence"). Trust me... this is a great read and there's so much to glean from Bob's learnings and his legacy. Thanks Bob for teaching me—this book is a gift to youth workers."

— **DOUG FIELDS** YOUTH PASTOR, AUTHOR, CO-FOUNDER OF DOWNLOADYOUTH-MINISTRY.COM

Bob Johns is and has been everything the students of the world need: steady, consistent, creative, authentic and, did I mention steady! In a world of "revolving door" youth ministry, Bob's longevity is rare and his perspective invaluable. I have watched Bob lead "up close," worked beside him and known him for decades...*They Say I'm Crazy*, is an indispensable guide for anyone seeking to influence this generation of students."

— **LOUIE GIGLIO** PASTOR OF
PASSION CITY CHURCH

When it comes to youth ministry, Bob Johns is a legend! Bob was someone who believed in me and my music long before anyone knew any of my songs. I am forever grateful to him for giving a young kid like me a chance to sing and lead worship at so many of his events. And this is the heart of youth ministry, believing in people. It's about time Bob wrote this book. I am so thrilled to recommend this book *They Say I'm Crazy*... a perfect title for anyone whose ventured in the treacherous waters of youth ministry."

— **CHRIS TOMLIN** SINGER,
SONGWRITER

# THEY SAY I'M CRAZY

*Going the Distance in Youth Ministry*

## BOB JOHNS

DTP, Waco, TX

ISBN 978-0-578-79943-8

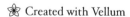 Created with Vellum

*For my Family*

# CONTENTS

# FOREWORD

It would be easy to call Bob Johns the "Methuselah of Student Ministry". But the truth is, Methuselah would have died much earlier if he had been a youth pastor. Besides that, we're pretty sure Bob went to elementary school with Methuselah and so that wouldn't be cool to compare him to an old classmate.

In January of 1988, Bob Johns invited us to his church to perform skits at a youth event. This would be the first gig the Skit Guys would ever perform outside our home church. In fact, we weren't even called "The Skit Guys". At that point we called ourselves "The E.T. Show". Bob's first advice to us was to reconsider our name. He said it this way, "You guys are funny but that name is stupid." We got his subtle message and changed our name straight away.

None of us really knew what we were getting into

that fateful weekend. It wasn't just a gig. It was the beginning of a lifelong friendship. We would both have Bob come speak to the students at the churches we served at as youth pastors. Bob would continue to invite us to his church, his camp, his daughter's birthday parties, and one unforgettable "Hoop-De-Do". (The name says it all.)

We both met our wives through Bob's ministry, he performed both of our marriage ceremonies, and Eddie even spent time working with Bob as his associate youth pastor.

Proverbs 4:7 says, *"The first step to becoming wise is to look for wisdom."* We believe that what you hold in your hands is a book of wisdom about student ministry and at the end of the day, about life. We have ministered alongside Bob. We have watched Bob minister year after year after year after year. He is the picture of what it looks like to be a faithful minister. On top of that, he's really good at what he does. One of the best. He has a shepherd's heart. He is creative. He seemingly transcends generations and is at the same time, the coolest old school person you could ever meet.

There is no chance that any of us are going to live long enough to gain the experience Bob has written in this book.  So do yourself a favor and read it from cover to cover. Highlight things, circle them in red, underline the stuff that hits you hard. We really believe this is one of those books you will keep handy and go back to year after year until you too have served in student ministry four score and seven years.   (BTW...we're pretty sure Bob went to college with that guy.)

Tommy & Eddie
    The Skit Guys

# INTRODUCTION

Hi, I'm Bob, and I've been working with teenagers my entire adult life. Trust me, it's been a long time. So I decided to write a book. First off, I want to state that this is not a memoir. My idea, from the very beginning, was to give encouragement and counsel on how to work with students over the long haul (and stuff that I think will be helpful no matter in what stage of life you might find yourself). Of course, I'm using a ton of life experience to back up the points I'll be making in this book. Now, if you're just getting started with youth ministry, put this book away and get yourself a copy of Doug Fields' excellent treatise called *Your First Two Years In Youth Ministry*. Why? First off, what a great book that is. All youth workers, no matter what stage of ministry they might be, should read that book. Second of all, this book you hold now will not be one on how to do youth ministry. Surely, every book ever needed in that area has been written by now—most of them by Doug. Rather, this is a book that goes into the little nuances, the less obvious nooks and crannies of this blessed and unbelievably cool occupation of working with youth. It's just some of the stuff that has bounced around in my cranial cavity for all these many years. So why not spew it out onto the written page? It's the stuff that pretty much kept me going to this crazy point of my life—still working with kids and enjoying it.

Of course, you should always love your family. Put them first right behind God. You should always recruit and nourish great volunteers. Always be a great planner. Don't forget to do your best to be organized, no matter how right-brained you might be. Remember the parents, and always pay close attention to your own personal spiritual journey. These are staples of effective youth ministry, and it wouldn't be right not to mention them in any book written about this subject. Consider them mentioned. I will not be covering these timely and critical subjects in these pages.

So anyway...hopefully, you'll find something beneficial in this book—a little something to assist you as you continue working with these crazy kids. I sure hope so. By the way, many of the names in this book have been changed for obvious reasons. Many have not.

## ONLY A FOOL

*"Even when no one else approved,*
*he took the job only a fool would do."*
Geoff Moore

The original skaters emerged in the 1960s. I was one of them. We made our own skateboards and immediately started doing extreme stuff without benefit of helmets or pads. I don't think any of those safety measures had been invented yet. One day, my friends and I took four wooden picnic benches and lined them up, end to end, down a hill for a little elevated ride—and quickly ended up in the emergency room. I was sure I had my first broken arm. It was definitely something only a fool would do. I'm sure my parents were thinking that.

Of course, extreme has taken on a new meaning in this day and time. I watch kids do those full 360s on skateboards, snowboards, even motorcycles, and I think, "Are they crazy?" Of course they're crazy. Just watch some of their mishaps on YouTube. It's probably not appropriate behavior to laugh out loud and cringe at the same time at all the extreme pain and suffering featured on those delectable videos. I just can't help myself.

Psychologist Michael Bradley revealed how nuts they are in his most excellent book, *Yes, Your Teen Is Crazy!*[1] He points out that there is still actual physiological development occurring in the brains of adolescents that gives explanation to much of their seemingly unexplainable behavior. So that gives some sense of understanding as to why a kid would throw an apple up in the air and try to catch it with his teeth. I've seen this with my own two eyes. He did it on his fifth or sixth try, complete with a bloody lip and a great sense of pride. Nuts! Maybe a little brain damage still there.

Now many people would say that only a fool would spend his or her life working with kids. That it's crazy! Oh it's a great thing to do while you're young and inexperienced, doing some meaningful ministry while building up the old resumé. But how many bunk beds and van rides and all-nighters can one person manage in a lifetime? Isn't there a limit? Maybe we should just pay our dues early and then while away the bulk of our adult ministry years sleeping in our own beds and going to lots of committee meetings.

Sitting in a seminary class in 1976, I was introduced to this idea of youth ministry as its own bona fide calling. I remember seeing it written on the chalkboard (by a fellow named Bob Taylor)—this idea that you could actually spend your life working with kids. This almost chimerical concept that youth ministry was not necessarily just a stepping stone to some other loftier ministerial position was groundbreaking stuff. Surely it would have been much better if we just got some experience and then moved up to something that was more prestigious and better paying. That was the same year that I truly felt God calling me into a ministry to students. All these many years later that call could not be any clearer. How many times have people with good intentions asked me what I was going to do when I grew up?

I remember coming to my present church at the age of 32 and concern being voiced about my age. Over three decades later and still at the same church, that sounds inane. Why not? Who said a person can't work with youth that are generations removed from them? Of course, the thought of someone eligible for the senior discount at the movies ministering to those using student IDs to get the same discount sounds pretty ludicrous as well. Actually it sounds crazy.

. . .

## The Job Only A Fool Would Do

Has there ever been a time when students were more clueless about career choices than now? I don't think so. I've talked with plenty who are in an all-out search for that elusive vocation – the one that pays the bills but still offers tons of fulfillment. Of course, parents are just hoping that their well-educated offspring can finally pick up the car and hospitalization insurance. That can be kind of hard when you have a college degree, student loans out the wazoo, and still making lattes for a living. But when that day arrives, when you finally figure out what you want to do with your life, it's one of the best days ever. I've seen that look in someone's eyes when the vocational pathway suddenly becomes obvious. Life just begins to make sense.

A long, long time ago that happened to me. My home church invited me to become their first part-time youth minister. Up to that moment, I was floundering, with a college degree and absolutely no sense of direction. The pastor recognized something in me that I didn't see in myself. I think it might have been when he saw me impressing a group of junior high guys by chugging a two-liter bottle of Big Red. (To this day, I can't stand Big Red.) Or it might have been something else. Still I took the job and by the end of the first month, I knew! I think it was why it was so easy for me to embrace this new paradigm for youth ministry—a calling in and of itself. This was not a calling with strings attached to do this until you get promoted up the ranks to something better. I loved it, couldn't get enough of it, and never looked back.

A few years ago, the folks at Youth Specialties used a song by Geoff Moore as their theme for their youth workers convention. It was perfect for such a gathering as this. They even took time during one of the general sessions to call all the 20-year plus veterans up on the stage for a bit of recognition. They presented us with court jester hats and proclaimed to all in the arena that we were a bunch of fools. We donned them proudly as Geoff sang. The song was *Only A Fool*, and the words were simple, yet profound:

Charlie was a fool
Did you hear what he went and did?
He quit his job, threw it away
Gave his life to a bunch of kids
He said he was in love with Jesus
But his friends didn't understand
He could've had it all
But he just smiled and said
That he already did.
He saw the big in the small
He saw the beauty in the call
Even when no one else approved
He took the job only a fool would do.[2]

. . .

The big in the small—a lovely paradox from the mind of Geoff Moore. What has often been considered small, not as significant, just a stage, is actually bigger than we could ever imagine. But if you're not looking for it, you will probably miss it. I've heard it theorized that the reason many of the churches in England are struggling so much today is because they missed a generation. The church became so irrelevant that its young people turned away and never looked back. A generation was lost and so was almost all the spiritual momentum that persisted so predominately in the 1950s. It could be entirely possible and makes great sense to me that the leadership didn't see the big in the small. They looked right past the small and never made the gospel relevant to an emerging youth culture. Just wondering.

Jesus talked about this very thing in Matthew 18:6: *But whoever causes one of these little ones who believe in Me to sin, it would be better for him to have a great millstone fastened around his neck and to be drowned in the depth of the sea.* [3]

You could make a really good case for these "little ones" referenced as being teenagers (or at least pre-teens). They definitely have to be old enough to have reached an age of accountability. How else could you cause one to stumble unless they were fully aware of sin? These are strong words to anyone who might overlook the bigness of these little ones. Talking about being a fool. To have a heavy millstone hung around your neck is probably a reference to the stone that a donkey would push to grind mill, carrying the weight day after day, exerting the force to keep the stone moving ever circular, never arriving anywhere different. What a grind! What a punishment meted out for the one who would ever cause one of these little ones to stumble!

It's one thing to intentionally cause someone to stumble. The Greek word for stumble is *skandalizo*, which strangely resembles our word scandalize. Sounds like something real premeditated—like the horrid stories of youth pastors who sexually violate one of the lambs from their flock. I hear those stories all too often, and it always brings out a sense of vigilantism within me. May the millstones around the necks of these lecherous creeps be the heaviest available.

But I don't really think it's a stretch to say that this could refer simply to the act of ignoring or failing to consider these seemingly insignificant ones. Everyone with any sense of decency wants to reach kids for Christ—that is, as long as it doesn't get out of control, stays real orderly, doesn't leave any holes in the sheetrock, and leaves worship unfettered by too many of those non-hymnal choruses. Too often, salaries and budgets reflect this lack of acknowledgement, and the only real attention can be summed up in the simple words, "Turn it down!" I guess bad attention is better than no attention, right? So who is foolish enough to want to reach out to these little ones, especially for the long haul?

## The Beauty in the Call

I was leading a caravan of vehicles along the Baja Peninsula from Ensenada, Mexico to San Diego. We were returning from a mission trip and really enjoying the spectacular drive along the Pacific coast. There were some islands just a few miles out that we could see in the distance. I threw it out there. "Look! Someone told me on a clear day you could see Hawaii from this road." I waited for the laughter that was sure to come, but I got something I hadn't counted on. Michelle and Shawna both started saying things like "Really!" "That's Hawaii?" "That's so cool!" Only Michelle was a blonde, but both were playing the part. Everyone else quickly caught on, and we carried on the charade for many more miles. There were even pictures taken, as suppressed laughter threatened to overflow the van at any moment. I really can't remember if I ever clued the girls in on their misconception. Maybe I should look them up and explain that the Hawaiian Islands are 2,700 miles across the Pacific Ocean from Mexico.

No matter how much the girls believed those islands seen with the naked eye were the islands of

Hawaii, it wasn't true. Even if they trusted that their youth minister would never try to deceive them and believed him unequivocally, it could never be true. Islands off the Pacific coast of Mexico, words from a trusted advisor, bogus words of confirmation from surrounding friends—it all adds up. To one employing her reasoning skills, it makes great sense. It must be true. It just feels right.

Isn't that an apt description of the way truth is being handled in these days of our lives? Like sands in the hourglass, so does objective truth seem to be slipping through the fingers of these little ones. It's like the cartoon that showed a boy at the chalkboard in class. He had written the simple mathematical equation, $2 + 2 = 5$. The caption said it all: "I know it's not right. It's just how I feel."

That's the beauty in the call. Extremely difficult, yet so beautiful is the call to come alongside of students and join them in the journey through the wonderland of right beliefs. Of course along the way, there will be voices pointing out islands of twenty-first century wisdom and sophistication. To the highly impressionable observer, it would just have to be right or at least plausible. "Maybe 2 plus 2 really is 5. I don't know. Sounds like it could be true." To stand at that crossroads and to serve as a counselor and a guide to real truth is a magnificent calling, a beautiful place in which to find oneself.

· · ·

## We Have This Ministry

Comedian Steven Wright says that half the people you know are below average. He also says that 42.7 percent of all statistics are made up on the spot. Sometimes it really feels that way. Now I've quoted this following statistic often throughout the years, and as I do so now, I must qualify that I can't find the source. But here it is anyway: 85% of people who come to Christ, do so by the time they turn 18. I've thrown this around to justify my claim that youth ministry was where the action is. I would always reiterate that if we don't lead them to Jesus before they graduate from high school, most will never follow that path. That's a good one to use when you're trying to get the finance committee to up your youth budget. Whether this statistic is right on, severely dated, or just plain fiction, the point is well made. This is where the action is; most will not encounter Christ if we miss them during this important station of life.

The real beauty of the call is when the call is for a lifetime. How many times have I watched youth workers flounder because it really wasn't their call? Gifted, yes! Called, no! The results were often short-lived and non-reproducing. I would trade charisma and hilarity for calling every time. When the laughter fades and the bag of tricks starts to run low, the gifted minister (who is looking forward to the next promotion) becomes dissatisfied, even as the kids and volunteers start to wonder why.

The Apostle Paul opens up the fourth chapter of 2 Corinthians with these words, *"Therefore, since we have this ministry, as we received mercy, we do not lose heart."* [4] I like the words, we have this ministry. God called Paul out of a life of hatred and destruction to a ministry of reconciliation. His commitment to that calling has been well chronicled and basically unparalleled. If there was ever anyone who had the right to lose heart in his calling, it had to be Paul. Comparing a scathing email from an angry parent (because his daughter left an event early and didn't get a t-shirt) with the beating that Paul took is ludicrous. The big difference is it seems that Paul didn't seem to ever lose heart – and we...well it does seem a bit silly, doesn't it?

We have this ministry, entrusted to us by the Heavenly Father, and are called to finish the job assigned to us. Matthew 9 reveals the mind-boggling compassion of Jesus: Seeing the people, He felt compassion for them, because they were distressed and dispirited like sheep without a shepherd. Then He said to His disciples, *"The harvest is plentiful, but the workers are few. Therefore beseech the Lord of the harvest to send out workers into His harvest."* [5] The Greek word used here for compassion is a strong one. The definition: to be moved as to one's bowels. My good friend,

Dawson McAllister, said it simply meant to see something that made you almost throw up. Add to that a sense of urgency to do something about what made you sick to your stomach, and you have a powerful definition of the compassion of Christ. It could be reasoned that upon seeing the multitudes, He was moved so deeply and sickened by how beat down they were, that He felt this urgent need to do something.

When I read this passage, I always think about the hallways in the high schools and middle schools where our students attend. When that bell rings, those hallways quickly fill up with multitudes of teenagers. If we could see them the way Jesus sees them, maybe we could have a deeper sense of urgency about these sheep without a shepherd, about these distressed and dispirited individuals who are so spiritually needy. Jesus points out astutely that the workers are few. Maybe it's because too many forsake that call and move on to something more measurable and much more 8 to 5 in nature.

I am not here to try to talk people into committing to youth ministry for life. But I am here to state the obvious. Better yet, let Jesus do the talking, *"The harvest is plentiful, but the workers are few."* Why? Maybe because too many think of youth ministry as a stop on the way to a higher calling. I've had many friends who left youth ministry for other positions and most, initially, didn't really like what they were doing. In fact, a common theme was that there was something missing – it seemed less than satisfactory. I was always quick to point out, in my most condescending voice, that they probably screwed up and shouldn't have left the lovely and fulfilling opportunity they had to work with kids for a living. I would pontificate about the joys of youth ministry and the glaring shortcomings of their newly chosen profession. They probably didn't enjoy hearing me talk (not nearly as much as I enjoyed it) and didn't appreciate me using my spiritual gift of sarcasm in such a way, but there was often an awkward silence that ensued. I really think that some of my former colleagues chose poorly.

So it is really possible? Can you really work with kids, even as you maneuver your way through your own midlife crisis? Let's face it. How much pizza is one person actually supposed to eat over the course of a lifetime? Is a lifelong calling to ministry with students just a pipe-dream? I think not. So how can one go the distance in youth ministry? The following chapters are not really a how-to book on youth ministry. Those are plentiful. These are words that capture the essence of how one can make the long run and do marathon youth ministry for a lifetime. It's just some thoughts and ideas I've discovered along the beautiful pathway of my lifetime in youth ministry—some of the principles and passions that have enabled me to joyfully keep my focus. As you read, maybe you'll find something useful.

# Chapter Two

# THE MORE THINGS CHANGE, THE MORE THEY REMAIN THE SAME

*"There comes a time in every man's life
and I've had plenty of them."*
Casey Stengel

A few years ago, I was sitting in Starbucks when this 20-something young lady walked in. She was dressed attractively, almost conservatively, business-like—probably in pharmaceutical sales. (How many of those people are there?) But she had a rather sizeable tattoo on her back, stretching between her shoulder blades. Her top covered it, sort of. I thought to myself, doesn't she represent the postmodern mindset that sees tattoos as a perpetual accessory, the kind that keeps giving? Then I begin to wonder. . .

She's possibly very spiritual, but hates Bush and

the war in Iraq (I told you this was a few years ago), sees absolutely nothing wrong with same sex marriage, could be pro-choice and pro-God. But she may not be a big fan of the institutional church. And then it hit me...I was exactly like that when I was her age, minus the tattoo.

When I was in my 20s, I was extremely spiritual. (I remember some of the most passionate times of prayer and my worn-out Living Bible.) But I hated the Vietnam War and Nixon. My tattoo was my long hair and far out clothes. And was I ever a critic of the church. Of course, I was there every Sunday, but I saw what I thought was clearly the lack of relevance in an institution marred by an undeniable bourgeois tendency—passionate about orderly services and potluck dinners, equally dispassionate about anything messy, uncommon, or uncomfortable. It was a meticulously sought-after place of mediocrity. But it was the 70s and change was saturating the atmosphere. You could feel it. You could see it.

One day it hit me: I've worked with students during five decades. That's right, add 'em up – the '70s, the '80s, the '90s, and now two decades and counting into the twenty-first century. I started back when there was a lot of really good music, hair was really long (mine was shoulder length or longer), and youth culture was in full bloom. We could set up a volleyball net, mix up some Kool-Aid, and have scores of bell-bottom clad teens pop in for the occasion. I can actually remember playing *Amazing Grace* to the tune of *House of the Rising Sun* on my guitar for youth group. And everybody thought it was so cool. Larry Norman became the poet laureate for a new generation of believers, singing "You say all men are equal, all men are brothers...Then why are the rich more equal than others?"[1] We heard this stuff, totally freaked out, and began to rally around a new kind of Christianity.

We started hauling guitars and drums into the church, whereupon the deacons put out their cigarettes on the front porch and begin their line of defense against these hippies that threatened the church's traditions. I remember one church that refused to let our group come perform a youth musical for their congregation because some of our guys had long hair. We were some of the very first modern day, cultural martyrs—which was very, very cool. It was quite the hip time to live. Researcher Merton Strommen surveyed the scene and announced that this new generation was boldly crying out in social outrage, while also slipping on a tie-dyed t-shirt emblazoned with the logo of self-gratification. It certainly seemed that the residue of the unprecedented 60s protest against all things considered establishment (especially war on the other side of the globe) had carried over to some extent. The church would most definitely be affected by it, no doubt.

The '80s came along and the sense of entitlement began to come full bloom. It was the decade when "If it feels good, do it!" actually became a reality. Music took a turn for the worse. MTV was partly to blame. How else could Duran Duran ever have made it? But it was, in my humble opinion, the absolute best decade for movies. Luke finally wooed his father over from the dark side. Marty took us back to the future. Indiana made archeology cool. Rocky beat Apollo, Clubber, and that big Russian dude. And Maverick defied authority and still ended up being top gun. Bangs were really big and fluffy, and mullets (yes, I had one and it was very cool) threatened to take over the world. Baggy t-shirts were in, which was also very cool. I only ordered large and extra-large tees for camp and no one complained. Wow, that's one thing that really changed and now is changing back. For a while, I was ordering a kazillion smalls and one XL for myself. Now the bigger sizes are back. I'm very grateful. If you have to order tees on a regular basis like me, the changing in sizes may be the most difficult of changes to keep up with. Let's face it, t-shirt business is very stressful. Anyway, back to the '80s. Toward the end of the decade, Reagan made the verbal throw-down, "Mr. Gorbachev, tear down this wall." And two years later, the wall came tumbling down. And so did the cold war.

Youth ministry was still reaping the benefits from the revolution of the previous decade. Some pretty

books about how a thing called social media was going to change everything. Facebook made its entrance in 2003, and that's all I need to say about that for now. Maybe that's the biggest, most impactful change of them all. In addition, reality television has taken over the world. Hip-hop just will not go away. Hoodies, tight jeans, holey jeans, baggy jeans that droop to impossible depths, tight shirts, floppy shirts, flip flops (no matter the wind chill factor) are all fashion statements coming at the beginning of this new era. But history will more than likely place the bookend on the start of this new millennium as being the events of 9/11. War has gotten messy again and keeps popping up in innocent places. Families are more fractured than ever. Kids actually cut themselves just to escape pain. And the need for sincere community, which has always been there, is greater than ever.

### The Times They Are A-Changin'

In Dylanesque fashion, we can say "the times they are a-changin'," and doing so in rapid-fire succession. This brings us to the title of this chapter: The more things change, the more they remain the same. This paradoxical saying attributed to Alphonse Karr (some French dude) seems silly at first, definitely trite and a bit cheesy in the least, and indefensible for sure. So could it possibly be true? I think so.

One day, I received a text message from Bonnie, who was one of my seniors at the time. It read, "Bob, thanks for being there during our prime suffering years." It was a nice gesture from her, but not necessarily original. She was quoting from the movie *Little Miss Sunshine* where Steve Carrell's character counseled his nephew that high school is the time of prime suffering years. He goes on to say, "You don't get better suffering than that." Throughout the years, change has been substantial to say the least, but the needs, the struggles, the suffering, and the solutions have remained basically the same. Of course, the ante has been raised with such, heretofore, unheard of issues like eating disorders and self-mutilation. But there have always been families that are dysfunctional and broken relationships and abuse and drugs and loneliness and pressures to conform. And suffering...

It was twenty years ago—the question on the sheet said, rather playfully, "What is one talent or ability you wished you had?" One girl wrote, "To become invisible." She was sitting in my office. I quipped that it would be a lot of fun to be able to make yourself invisible. You know—sneak into concerts, listen in on conversations, rummage through the senior pastor's office, scare the living daylights out of friends. She didn't laugh, didn't even smile. "I wish I could become invisible, just to see if anybody would notice if I was gone." As she said this, she dug her fingernails into her hand to the point that it made me cringe. She felt less than zero. And I truly felt compassion for her plight. There is no debate that the prime suffering years of loneliness and self-hatred have remained the same.

Rock oddity, David Bowie has a song appropriately titled "Changes" which talks about ripples in a stream that are constantly changing, even as the days are always the same. Then he adds terrific insight about children who are trying to change the world they live in. These same children are "immune to your consultations", because they're pretty sure they know what they're doing. And the chorus goes, "Ch-ch-ch-changes – turn and face the strain. Ch-ch-ch-changes."[2] The ripples are changing in size, but never leaving the stream. The needs are shifting, intensifying, increasing, even diminishing. But the mighty river carries on, flowing on in due course, despite all the surface churning and unseen undercurrent. Ch-ch-ch-changes...still the days seem the same.

Once, another one of our girls actually said to a friend, "I think I'm gonna try out a new personality this week. The one I'm using right now isn't working for me." It was hard to believe these words were pouring forth from Susan's mouth. But then it really wasn't all that hard to believe. Throughout her prime suffering years, she had been in an all-out search for identity. Instead of being herself, she was pasting on bits and pieces of items picked up as she moved down the line of the identity smorgasbord—a little bit of this, a little bit of that. Susan was going to try the dumb blond routine. In her mind, it was obviously working for some of the girls in her school. It was funny and cute, and it just might be the personality for her.

Could that be the really big problem facing students, the problem that has remained the same throughout the decades? Did the problem of identity set the table for all other problems to thrive and take their toll? The kids keep trying to change their worlds to adjust to the changing world. That's why Xanga turned into Myspace which turned into Facebook which turned into Twitter which turned into Instagram which turned into Snapchat which turned into whatever. Whenever their parents invade something that was just theirs, they move on to something else—something that is uniquely theirs and provides some kind of expression and stability. I remember reading about some kid hanging himself from a tree in his backyard to which he had affixed a sign that read, "This tree is the only thing in my life that is stable." Too often, as Bowie put it, they are immune to our consultations.

## Tumbling Down the Rabbit Hole

Dwayne, the angst-filled teenager in *Little Miss Sunshine*, wore a t-shirt silk-screened with "Jesus was wrong" on the front. Obviously, I disagree with that statement. As I have presented Christ to students throughout these many years, I have been immersed in the process of helping students see that Jesus and the powerful claims of the Gospel are the solution. The problems have basically remained the same, even in the midst of mind-boggling change. Just go buy any kind of technology. By the time you get it home, unpacked, and set up, it's already obsolete. "Ch-ch-ch-changes...They are quite aware of what they're going through." It's a lot! But the solution has never, and will never change: Jesus Christ—the same yesterday, today, and tomorrow. Yes, to add to frustration, they often continue to be immune to Christ-filled consultations offered by those older and wiser, those who may actually know what they're talking about.

The older and wiser Preacher, at the end of his treatise on "telling us [as ministers] what we need not do—in fact, must not do,"[3] finishes with these words in Ecclesiastes. *The conclusion, when all has been heard, is: fear God and keep His commandments, because this applies to every person.*[4] What's he saying? Basically, "Been there, done that. So here it is, plain and simple—here's the key to life and life lived to the fullest extent." Still we often ignore the wisdom of this often overlooked Old Testament favorite.

Just like our kids. This older and possibly wiser youth minister still loves to ski, but I choose wisely now when it comes to "catching air" while skiing. Too much jumping leaves me aching all over, like those

Saturday mornings after playing in a football game in high school. We're talking—I can hardly get out of bed the next morning. By the way, this is all high school students think about while skiing—looking for jumps on every run. They're obsessed with it. When I'm skiing with the extreme generation, I will often ski ahead and scout the blind jump they all want to take. I can look over the ridge and signal to them that the landing area is clear for take-off. I use this illustration with them all the time, a reminder that it's smart to listen to those who have been down life's path before them. Life's perspective from those who have been there before, those who can clearly articulate what they are facing just beyond the ridge, should never be ignored as being irrelevant, but should be heeded as an invaluable piece of information. In fact, way back in 1952, C.S. Lewis wrote:

"Keep nothing back. There must be a real giving up of the self. You must throw it away 'blindly' so to speak—trying to forget about the self altogether. Your real, new self (which is Christ's and also yours, and yours just because it is His) will not come as long as you are looking for it. It will come when you are looking for Him. Does that sound strange? The same principle holds, you know, for more everyday matters. Even in social life, you will never make a good impression on other people until you stop thinking about what sort of impression you are making."[5]

. . .

To be consumed by what kind of impression you are making is one of life's ball and chains. But to be consumed by finding one's identity in Christ will provide emancipation from what enslaves you...the humongous problem of identity. Isn't that what we want to do with students more than anything? That has never changed!

The more things change, the more they remain the same. Still true. Okay, I know that my digital watch supposedly has as much computer power as NASA had at its disposal putting the first man in space. When those future prognosticators like Leonard Sweet write this kind of stuff, it gives me brain cramps. So much change—the technology is bulldozing its way through life—can't keep up, everyone keeps falling behind. Yikes! The change is tumultuous as it constantly clamors for our attention. But those very first astronauts were supposedly required during their training to put down twenty answers to the question, "Who are you?" Very interesting! In spite of the technological advances, the dire need for identity, purpose, and acceptance continually plagues the generations. It always will. That's what makes this job so arduous, yet so regal.

In *The Matrix*, Neo is offered the blue pill by Morpheus where, "the story ends, you wake up...and believe whatever you want to believe." Or he can take the red pill and "stay in Wonderland, and I'll show you how deep the rabbit hole goes." We get to go tumbling down the rabbit hole with students, helping them find real reality. Not a bad way to live, not a bad way at all. It's the search for identity, for what's real in a world that can be so synthetic. Someone once said, "Reality is a nice place to visit, but I sure wouldn't want to live there."

Helping kids leap into the blackness of faith and discovering the reality of Jesus Christ versus settling for the status quo or even inventing their own reality...that's the challenge that remains the same. Nothing else makes sense. The Psalmist said, *"Keep me safe, O God, I've run for dear life to You. I say to God, 'Be my Lord!' Without you, nothing makes sense."*[6] Oh yeah!

# Chapter Three

# MY TERRIFYING LITTLE SECRET

*O me! O life! Of the questions of these recurring*
*Of the endless trains of the faithless*
*Of cities filled with the foolish*
*What good among these, O me, O life?*
*Answer: That you are here*
*That life exists and identity*
*That the powerful play goes on*
*And you will contribute a verse.*
Walt Whitman

I have always had this terrifying little secret. It was one that was deep inside the castle of my soul, with the drawbridge drawn up so very securely. No one could ever know or even suspect this hidden truth about me. Because if I were ever exposed, everyone would discover what a fraud I was. It may not be what you might think. It could be one of the usual suspicions of those who are always looking for the dirt in most situations. But it's not. There are no provocative tales of lust or desire out of control. No hidden skeletons in the closet revealing predilections for the unusual or the creepy. I do relieve my nasal cavities of unnecessary obstructions while driving, but who doesn't do that? That's not it. I do enjoy watching *Dancing With The Stars* with my wife, a very unmanly thing to do. Not it either. I like to cheat at table games, just to see if I can get away with it. (To this day, my wife refuses to play some games with me.) A real flaw in my character, no doubt, but not the secret to which I'm referring. I often show up at graduations and other school events at the very end, just to be seen by kids and their parents. Not it. And in seminary, I signed numerous prophetic reading report forms, acknowledging books I had supposedly read—books that I have never, and will never read in their entirety. Okay, my integrity way back then was obviously a work in progress, but not the little secret either.

My terrifying little secret is the fact that I have always known deep inside how absolutely inadequate I am as a youth minister. There was always this nagging fear that one day I would be exposed for who I really was—a very ordinary, average, unskilled fellow who had no business leading a ministry like this. After 40 years, I still am either the biggest con artist since that *Catch Me If You Can* character or maybe, just maybe God has had His hand upon me (when I let Him) and was able to use me despite my inadequacies. The words in 2 Corinthians 12 remind us what Christ said to Paul, *"My grace is sufficient for you, for power is perfected in weakness."*[1] For Christ's sake, when I find myself weak (and fully acknowledge it), then I become strong. Because my dependence is upon the Strong One.

That means focusing on hearing God – not hearing the voices that say "useless," "spent," "out of sorts," "what's the point?" To be chained to these life-haters is to experience slavery that comes with a ball and chain. You drag it everywhere with you, grunting and groaning with the greatest of effort. It's being imprisoned by your own insecurity. And that has been my own personal prison throughout the years. Maybe it's been yours too.

I believe there's a fine line between debilitating insecurity, generated by the drive to avoid pain at all costs, and the admittance of inadequacy that drives you toward dependence upon the Father. One of my personal mottos has always been "No pain, no pain." Who likes pain? What I have discovered and what I have shared as counsel with many, is that the pain of short-circuited relationships can lead you down the path of self-protection. If you think about it, most of the wrong strategies we develop in life can be traced back to the subconscious drive to avoid even the appearance of pain.

## A 90-lb Theological Weakling

Some of my terror derives from the fact that I'm not that strong a theologian. If you throw me in the middle of the sea of systematic theology, there will be a lot of dog paddling to keep my head just above water. Oh there will be a few bold strokes here and there, but it's better if I remember to put on my hermeneutical floaties. Now I try to read thick books, but I will never be mistaken for a Bible scholar. Hey, I graduated from seminary about the same time that disco was heating up. When your tenure in youth ministry can be described like the Gettysburg's Address as two score and four years ago, you have to work really hard to keep your reading stout and your vocabulary from devolving down to the basic common denominator of "cool" and "dude" —two words that have most definitely stood the test of time. With these feelings of inadequacy rolling around in your skull, you can really get paranoid— expecting the church's personnel committee to come busting down your door one evening with really thick questions about the Pauline doctrine of Christ and demands for a listing of the minor prophets in the right order, or else!

On the other hand, the Psalmist said that the

hearts of the arrogant are covered with fat. What an apt description of the problem with arrogance. Now what does being a little haughty have to do with insecurity? Isn't it just a huge layer of psycho-cellulite built up to hide insecurity? I've been accused of being pretty cocky. Haven't we all? Without insecurity there is no need to parade your accomplishments or your skills. With insecurity the need is great. In your heart is reality—the good, the bad, the ugly—but covered with the "fat" of arrogance, of cockiness, of conceit. The problem is that too often reality gets reinvented.

I've seen some pretty brash youth workers. It has to be their fatness, putting on the pounds of arrogance. But reality...what is that? I was actually in an episode of a reality TV show about cheerleaders on TLC. (Trust me, if Reality TV ever shows up at your door, just say "No".) They had me reenact a real-life situation where I counseled one of my girls about a breakup. The words I shared with Katy were my words, good counsel, but were taken totally out of context—used by the producer to address a problem of which I was completely unaware. Through slick editing and total manipulation of the truth, they were able to create their own "reality." It's reality being reinvented once again. Let's be clear about one thing, there is no such thing as Reality TV—even my all-time favorite, *Duck Dynasty*, was so contrived. But I'm loving it! Think about it. If they were producing a show called "Youth Ministers Gone Wild"—and you, along with your friends, associates, parents, students, and family were all wired with a camera always trained on daily interactions, how would you not play to it? To at least some extent, it would be impossible not to do so. Thus, real reality would go out the window.

There is no doubt we can also reinvent ministerial reality as well. Just listen in on gatherings of ministers and you will often hear outbursts of arrogance about numbers and programs. It can be really hard not to join in with your own parade of accomplishments, waving your banner of "Look what I've done!" I intentionally try not to chime in on these displays of ministry exploits. But the temptation occasionally overcomes me, if not just to put some ostentatious braggart in his place. That's definitely my arrogance rearing its ugly head.

Maybe you can relate. That strange mixture of arrogance and insecurity can prove to be a personal prison for many on life's journey. Even now in my sixties, I haven't been able to break completely through these bars of confinement. To tunnel, for once and for all, through the fat walls of insecurity and to taste complete freedom (I mean Shaw-shankian-like freedom a la Andy Dufresne), still sometimes feels like a pipedream to so many. Just about the time you feel like the shackles have fallen off and freedom is within your grasp, some ninth graders will appear quite disinterested in your well-prepared, beautifully delivered talk, and you are once again at the mercy of your secret world. Or when some Hollister-wearing conformist made fun of my shoes once...I mean seriously, how often do you really look at a man's shoes?

To hear a rousing round of indifference to what you were sure was a hilarious anecdote, to see empty chairs at your regular youth meeting, to notice an intern snicker, quite innocently you hope, at your surefire idea for a t-shirt, these feed the monster. Then you start getting even older and face the fear of one day waking up and no longer being relevant. But I think that could be a good thing. I read in the brilliant *Bono in Conversation* about a time, right after their *Joshua Tree* album finally took U2 into superstar status, when bassist Adam Clayton suggested that the band take a well-deserved break. Bono retorted, "Break, we can't take a break. We're just a second away from being irrelevant."[2] Wow! I think all youth ministers should feel that sense of desperation about staying relevant. It just can't be allowed to be a fear monger. But we also can't let the pendulum swing to the arrogant side either.

Throughout my journals, there are constant references to Mr. Self-Reliant. That's what I call myself whenever my self-reliance becomes a liability. This could most certainly be viewed as a strength. It was self-reliance that qualified my father's generation to be labeled by Tom Brokaw as *The Greatest Genera-*

*tion.* (A must read by the way.) They pulled themselves up by their bootstraps after a great depression, and through a great war built a better America. Nothing wrong with that. Hey, self-reliance certainly enables one to be a great finisher. The stuff gets done—but too often of your own doing, with rolled up sleeves, tools in hand, and everyone saying a job well done. But it can so be a house of cards that you are trying to build. What has been wrought with your own hands, too often with token prayer and little direction from God, is a house of cards that will easily come crashing down at the slightest gust of wind. Self-reliance could eventually be the start of the dreaded downfall—all based in pride and false vanity. That's when you need to look in the mirror to see the face of a fully developing fool. Even when you're very aware of that fact, it's still hard to break away.

C.S. Lewis knew about this problem and wrote about it in *The Problem of Pain,* when he talked about the dangers of apparent self-sufficiency..."prostitutes are in no danger of finding their present life so satisfactory that they cannot turn to God: the proud, the self-righteous are in that danger."[3] So what you find is that your observable attribute of self-reliance can be the very thing that feeds the beast of your insecurity. When you hoist the entire task on your shoulders and pull it off, you do just that, but you've also managed to, once again, shove your ever-present insecurity back into the corner—under a pile of activities and accomplishments.

## One of the Beautiful People

I remember a study which revealed that beautiful people make bigger salaries than less beautiful people. I wondered how you could conduct such a survey. Didn't someone once say that beauty was in the eye of the beholder? My wife is still incredulous to the fact that as a young man I found Madeline Kahn (of *Blazing Saddles* and *Young Frankenstein* fame) quite attractive. So how did the surveyors determine who was beautiful and who was not? And then I wondered which category they would have put me in if I had been a participant. I think I know the answer to that one. I'm just not that pretty. And then I began to wonder if I would make more money if I were more beautiful. I didn't think so, but you never know.

If this is true, it's another indictment against a society that continues to place value on the perishable. I constantly warn our kids about doing this. They're all so young and beautiful, and they can really get caught up in the whole image deal. I will proclaim, "If you want to see what will happen to your body during the next forty years, look at me!" As I strike my best Zoolander pose, there is always a response of nervous laughter. I love how Mike

Yaconelli mused every year at the Youth Specialties conventions about reaching middle age and encountering sagging breasts, always with the quick follow-up, "And it happens to women too!" I always responded with my own nervous laughter.

Body image is not really that big a deal to me any more. I realize that's a lost cause, although I sometimes look in the mirror and am shocked at how old I look. I used to keep my membership at the Y, just because, even though I never went, I thought there was some psychological benefit from being a member of a health club. It's not the outside that can beat us up. It's the churning from within. I've already alluded to the fact that the pain of failed relationships can cause us to sometimes adopt wrong strategies for how we live. In the all-out attempt to avoid pain at all costs, we can subconsciously start living self-protected lives.

Sixteen-year-old Chuck had been adopted by his aunt and uncle and taken away from a dysfunctional situation where he was no longer wanted. Solid, great Christian family. Such a benevolent, gracious display of compassion. But now he was acting up, causing problems in the family, making some poor choices. The family called their church's youth minister to the rescue. A couple of things that happened during that family counseling session worth noting: there was the kid's reticent demeanor as his adoptive mother made this indicting statement, "Chuck, you know we told you when you came into our home that we could never love you as much as own children." There was also a poignant acceptance of this demonstration of conditional love from the lips of this adopted teen, "I know, Aunt Jerri." He was rescued from a hopeless place and put in another place that provided much love and security, yet quietly continued the assertion that he was not to be loved, or at least not as much as other, more deserving children. Thus, he was thoroughly in the mode of self-protection. Better bad attention than no attention at all. The negative behaviors were just visible acts coming from the short-circuited deep longing to be loved.

Hey, your insecurity isn't probably causing you to act up or cause trouble. You haven't been busted for public intoxication, and you probably haven't keyed any cars lately (although there may be a deacon's car you wouldn't mind leaving a mark on). But it can pull you into the self-protection foxhole just the same. But, really, I like to see it as a nerve ending that constantly reminds us we are thoroughly inadequate, absolutely bankrupt apart from God and His dunamis maximus.

This is never more distinct for me than when I perform a wedding. I do a lot of these stress-filled events, and this is the only thing that makes me nervous—that and the anxiety of using public transportation in big cities—oh, and also when I lose a couple of kids in the underground tube in London for about 45 minutes. I can do a wedding in our worship center for 200 people on a Saturday night and be as nervous as a long-tail cat in a roomful of rocking chairs—and then preach in that same building the next morning for 2,000 and be totally cool, calm, and collected. I've had a lot of ministers echo this same problem with weddings. I guess it's about the only thing we do that just has to be perfect. There is not much room for spontaneity as this bride looks to me to help her have a storybook ceremony. That's why I hit my knees in some empty Sunday School class-room in the minutes leading up to the big event. It's a good place to be—acknowledging your total depen-dence upon the Prince of Peace. You think I could figure out this would work in other areas of my life as well.

## Faith, Faith, Faith, You Gotta Have Faith

The Psalmist said it well, *"I love You, O Lord, my strength."*[4] How does one go about life without faith in God? There is such a fine line between sanity and the blackness of faithlessness. Sometimes during a sleep-less night when my insecurity takes on a power it could never possess during the waking hours, my thoughts reveal how easily the line is crossed over to hopelessness, despair—maybe even insanity. The temptation is to go throw down a tiny little cup of Nyquil and have sleep come on like a bandit—with the promise to steal away the weird, disproportionate thoughts that can only come during sleepless nights. How easily that line could be crossed. How easily one can lose perspective.

That's when it's a good time to turn to the Psalms, *"I love You, O Lord, my strength. [You're] my rock and my fortress and my deliverer."* When insecurity sucks life out of you, where can you go but to the Rock? *"My God, my rock, in whom I take refuge."* It's easy to think that some of the most blessed people are those who sleep well, seemingly content with their little place on this planet. How does one face the uncertainty of life when you feel that you're just about to topple over—or actually just taking that tiny step on to shifting sand that provides only temporary refuge and a foundation that is quickly cracking? I guess that's probably where the term "cracking up" came from.

*"My shield and the horn of my salvation, my stronghold."* God has got to be there. When we respond to tiny doubts that occasionally come to the forefront, we come to only one conclusion—it can only be true. What else makes sense? The horn of my salvation—to blow that horn makes sense in a world that many times makes none. We can spend a week in the mountains and not have one meaningful moment with God, and then stumble back into His stronghold on a sleepless night. Why? Why does He continue to take us back from our stumbling,

bumbling ways? He's God and we're not. He can take our insecurities and disintegrate them like a laser-zapped kidney stone—and what represented so much pain quietly moves along.

So there you have it, my terrifying little secret is out. I can strap it on like an artificial limb and lug it around as my albatross for life. Or I can allow it to thrust me into orbiting around my own self-reliance, masking the secret with the facade of complete self-confidence. One of my favorite authors, G.K. Chesterton, says that complete self-confidence is a weakness...and a sin! He continues:

> "Shall I tell you where the men are who believe most in themselves; For I can tell you. I know of men who believe in themselves more colossally than Napoleon or Caesar. I can guide you to the thrones of Super-men. The men who really believe in themselves are all in lunatic asylums. Believing that you have it all, everything you need to be a complete, self-sufficient person is living just one inch away from an awful emptiness. Believing in nothing will eventually leave you alone in your own nightmare - which will be like a cell with these words written over it, 'He believes in himself.'"[5]

Dude knows what he's talking about—and that was a hundred years ago. Or I can use it to my advantage, allowing me to stay in the faith dimension. There just doesn't seem to be much of a choice there. We'll see. I'm an extra ordinary poet, with extra emphasis on ordinary. But I wrote this once and found it in my journal. I think my old English teacher, Mildred Woodrum would be proud:

Daily the Great Emancipator
Proclaims freedom for this captive
And the chains tear away
Like those made by the fingers of children
From construction paper and staples
Ripped away as easily as that
Enslaved no more
Freedom like the wind in your face
Like a dance when no one's looking

# Chapter Four

# I'M ONE WILD 'N CRAZY GUY

*"A day without sunshine is like, you know, night."*
Steve Martin

In the 70s, in the midst of the rock and roll scene, came one Mr. Steve Martin. He was clean cut, always wore a suit, and without warning during his comedy act would exclaim, "I am one wild 'n crazy guy!" We laughed long and hard at this very unique style of stand-up. It was unpredictable, off the wall—it was wild 'n crazy. "Well excuuuuuse me!" became a part of the cultural vernacular. We all quoted him, maybe even tried to imitate his brand of humor in our daily interactions. He fretted over cat juggling, complained about the French having a different word for every-thing, and had us all repeating the Non-Conformists'

Oath. In fact, let's take a moment to do that right now. You'll be glad you did. Repeat after me: "I promise to be different! I promise to be unique! I promise not to repeat things other people say!"[1] Good!

What's the point? Throughout the years, I have continued to come across the occasional youth worker who has not, does not live up to the standards of the Non-Conformists' Oath. Being different. Being unique. Being yourself. Not trying to be something you're not. Like a wild 'n crazy guy. How many times have I met guys who are trying to be wild 'n crazy, when they really aren't? Now I've met some truly wild 'n crazy guys in my life. Like one of my former youth interns named Steve (not Martin) who could actually have people circle up and watch him dance at a wedding reception, like you see in a movie or something. It was not because he was a great dancer. It was just stinking funny. You know those kind of people. They have the guts and the brilliant sense of humor to pull that off. I'm really talking about the ones who try to pull that off, but it's so obviously disingenuous and always awkward.

I've often said, probably rather arrogantly, that I could spend thirty minutes with someone and tell if I thought they had the right stuff to do youth ministry. Once, I remember meeting the new youth minister from a sister church and knowing almost immediately that the church had made a mistake. We were at lunch with several local guys. From the start, he embarked on his wild 'n crazy routine, barking off one-liners and pulling off all his zany stunts with the awkwardness of a Michael Scott sensitivity training session. We were not amused. Why? Because it just wasn't him. There was nothing genuine about this self-introductory train wreck. He was a charlatan and was later terminated. I saw that one coming.

## The World Is Not a Stage

Shakespeare decreed that all the world was a stage, that we were merely actors involved in a grand universal performance. We don our costumes, apply make-up – all the time preparing to step from the wings into the spotlight. With the principal's permission, I remember going to a dance at the high school where most of the students in our ministry attend. I wore a costume. Not because I'm into that sort of thing—it was a Halloween dance. I had on a tux and a full head mask—one of those old man with the creepy smile type masks. For the next hour, I entered the real world of high school incognito. It was surreal. Nobody knew who I was, and I heard things that I hadn't planned on hearing. A student who came to lots of our stuff, looked intently into the eyes of my latex cover-up and incriminated himself, "Who in the 'bleep' are you?" – except he didn't use the word, 'bleep.' I thought to myself, if you only knew.

It's fun to dress up and pretend to be different characters. It's just important to remember that it's not reality. I was not, and never again will be a high school student, even if for a couple of hours, I acted like one. I will never forget when Tommy Woodard and Eddie James (of Skit Guys fame) went with me to pick up Al Denson (of B the 1 fame) at the San Diego airport. This was obviously back when I wore a younger man's clothes. We were doing a camp in that fantastic city, and Al was doing a concert that evening. Tommy had decided to dress up as Arnold Schwarzenegger's Terminator character, as part of a prank on Al (later this would come to be referred to as being *Punk'd*). As we came out into the parking lot, Terminator Tommy runs up and grabs Al's dress bag off the Skycap's cart. Whereupon, said Skycap began an active and quite effective pursuit of TT, placing him in an inescapable headlock. This was serious stuff, and still Tommy kept muttering in his best Schwarzenegger accent, "I'll be back." I finally had to get down on one knee, look him in the eye, and state rather sharply, "Tommy, it's time to break character." If you know Tommy, breaking character is hard for him to do. But he finally acquiesced to what could have become a dicey situation. He stopped the pretense.

Dressing up and playing a character is one thing, but pretending to be something you're not in everyday, real life is another. I guess one way to describe it would be hypocrisy. The word hypocrite originates from a Greek theatrical term, literally meaning "to answer from under a mask." The original usage was in reference to an orator or one who interprets dreams. But the word eventually devolved to the negative connotation that we are most familiar with today – coming to refer to people who present themselves as something they're not. Like Shakespeare put it, "God has given you one face, and you make yourself another."[2]

As has always been the case, some choose to place themselves into the role of determining who the hypocrites are. But Don Marquis pointed out, "A hypocrite is a person who – but who isn't?" Truth be known, we are all hypocrites. The Message's interpretation of Matthew 6:1-4 pictures Christ putting it like this:

> "Be especially careful when you are trying to be good so that you don't make a performance out of it. It might be good theater, but the God who made you won't be applauding. When you do something for someone else, don't call attention to yourself. You've seen them in action, I'm sure 'playactors' I call them— treating prayer meeting and street corner alike as a stage, acting compassionate as long as someone is watching, playing to the crowds. They get applause, true, but that's all they get. When you help someone out, don't think about how it looks. Just do it—

quietly and unobtrusively. That is the way your God, who conceived you in love, working behind the scenes, helps you out." [3]

## Piece Or Not A Piece?

This is really much more than a discussion of the wild 'n crazy. It's about authenticity in relationships. Being authentically who you are, the way God wired you, is one of the great gifts you can give your kids. It's like e.e. cummings said, "it takes courage to grow up and become who you really are." But many grown-ups still live in the world of pretentiousness, building daily on the facade of the fake and synthetic.

I rounded the corner into our church's foyer area one Sunday morning and saw a fellow I knew quite well sporting his brand new toupee. I immediately and chicken-heartedly did a one-eighty and walked away in search of another route to get where I needed to go. Why? Because I realized one of the great unanswered questions in this life is...what do you say to someone who suddenly, without warning, dons a hairpiece? One day a chrome dome, the next a head full of someone else's hair. Do you draw attention to it? "Hey, nice piece, looks so natural" (lie). Or do you act like you didn't notice that all of a sudden he has a ridiculous piece of shag carpet on his head? I still don't know the answer to that question. If you wear a piece, that's your business. I can't imagine why, but that's between you and your loved ones. I am fairly sparse in the upstairs hair department. It's the age-old problem of having hair grow where I don't want it, and not having it grow where I deeply desire it. And I have thought it would be the very best gag if I could ever get my hands on a toupee and show up one day proudly spouting a head full. Just to watch the response of others, as I acted seriously about my new cover-up, would be absolutely priceless.

Now it's one thing to affix a toupee to keep oneself from growing more face. It's another to affix the unnatural to your personality, to insincerely mimic other approaches to relating and communicating— even with the best intentions. Years ago, a Baylor University ministerial student kept promoting himself to me as a possible speaker at our midweek high school meeting. I liked him, despite the fact that he kept parading his resumé of recent speaking engagements in an attempt to impress me. So I invited him to come and do his thing. He showed up that night. This will tell you how long ago this was, because he was wearing suspenders that matched his red Chuck Taylor's. For your information, that was cool back then. We sat on the front row and quietly visited a bit throughout the first part of the program. Then I introduced him and invited him to the stage. That was when the unexpected happened. He stepped up and immediately busted out his preacher voice. You know what I'm talking about. That projected tone with the evangelistically-induced pronunciation, that unnatural waver in the voice that is so artificial, so mimicry. I sat there sulking in incredulity as I allowed my students to be subjected to such an ostentatious display, feeling quite helpless to do anything about it.

Thomas Merton said it well when he postulated, "Our interior word must be more than an echo of the words of someone else. There is no point in being a moon to somebody else's sun, still less is there any justification for our being moons of one another, and hence darkness to one another, not one of us being a true sun."[4] If we go around echoing and imitating, we miss the mark totally. To be a moon to somebody's else's sun is to miss out on the very reason you were born. U2's Bono talked about when he came to the realization that "the two big events of your life, which is your birth and your death, you don't have any say over."[5] We may not have much control of those two huge moments, the bookends of our physical existence. But someone else stated that the two great moments in life are the moment you were born and the moment you realize why you were born. So we do have a say on the issue of why we were born— why God put us here...and how we should search out being a moon to God's Son.

A hairpiece is so easily identified. It's almost like a neon sign illuminating the obvious. I remember when Letterman did a bit called "Piece Or Not A Piece" –

where they went on the street and videotaped suspected wig-wearers. Dave and Paul would try to decide if the man's locks were real or made up. They were rarely wrong. If you've worked with kids for any length of time at all, you know that they can usually spot a "piece" from a mile away. They're pretty good at spotting someone who is faking it. But not always. Of course, you know within your own soul when you're faking it. Almost 100% of the time. Long lasting, durable, and useful ministry will not be in the works for the one who doesn't realize that. Enunciating your words like Louie Giglio or using Matt Chandler's dramatic pauses won't make you more effective. You'll just have your listeners wondering, "Is that a piece he's wearing?"

## Exaggeration Is To Paint A Snake And Add Legs

It's one thing to mimic a good communicator – it's another to lack integrity in the process. A defining moment in my ongoing development as a minister happened in the late '80s. I was at a modest youth ministers' conference in the Dallas/Fort Worth metroplex. The most unassuming, seemingly uncool guy got up to speak to the 150 or so youth ministers. His name was Dave Busby. Maybe you've heard of him. Maybe not. He passed away in December of 1997, six months before he was supposed to do our camp for the fourth or fifth time. This was after battling cystic fibrosis his entire life. He was scrawny, unhealthy looking, wore an ill-fitted sports coat and tie, and I began to exercise my other spiritual gift of cynicism as I prepared myself not to be impressed. Little did I know that I was about to be introduced to the one of God's great spokespersons for this time and place.

He proceeded to blow us away with a little talk he had entitled "Fatal Flaws." I still have the notes I took from that day. He described a fatal flaw as a seemingly small spiritual hiccup that could lead to one becoming a spiritual fatality. It was a prophetic word if I've ever heard one. He talked about several instances of these fatal flaws, but the one that established a permanent residence in the spiritual journal that is etched on my heart was the one about exaggeration.

Remember Ananias and Sapphira in Acts 5? They sold their property and gave part of the proceeds to the church. Pretty admirable to say the least. One problem, of course, is that they both, at separate occasions, exaggerated about the amount. First, Ananias laid what he said was the full amount received from the sale at the feet of the apostles. A small embellishment, a slight misrepresentation, a tiny flaw in the presentation...the result was fatal. Literally, the last thing he heard in this life was Peter saying, "You have not lied to men but to God." Then later here comes Sapphira, totally unaware of the lethal implications of her complicity. Peter even gives her a chance to speak the truth, "Now what was that price again?" She stuck with her story and paid dearly as well. "That is the price." Peter immediately points to the young men who will momentarily remove her dead body from the premises – like her husband before her.

Now that's what I call a fatal flaw. Busby told a story revealing what a complete, transferable concept that biblical story was. He was leading a conference on the Holy Spirit and had actually spent right at one hundred hours studying in preparation for the event. During one of the sessions, he exaggerated that fact. He made a quick reference to the fact that he had studied for "hundreds of hours" in preparation for the conference. You know how you can be speaking to a group and be thinking about something else at the same time. That happened to me once when I was preaching in "big" church. I suddenly became concerned that I had forgotten to zip my pants, which turned out to be true. I actually stood behind the pulpit and quietly addressed the wardrobe malfunction without missing a beat in delivering my sermon. But I digress.

Dave said that at that moment the Holy Spirit quizzed him, "Did you say hundreds of hours?" All the time while continuing to speak to the gathering, he responded defensively to the Spirit that he meant to say "a hundred hours" but that "hundreds" was close to the truth. They had a brief debate over the slight misrepresentation, and then he proceeded to blow past God's conviction and continue his presentation. At that point, Dave said he finished his well-prepared, well-delivered talk under his own power, without the Spirit's presence and power. After a night of tossing and turning, he stood before the group the next evening and confessed his exaggeration, asking their collective forgiveness for his indiscretion. Now that's what I call spiritual integrity.

As we embark into the foolishness of preaching the gospel, it really is foolish to cloud the issue with our own silly attempts to bolster the message with our embellishments. It's like the message isn't strong enough and interesting enough unless we punch some life into it. So the illustration gets a little more dramatic, and the results a bit more impressive, and the conclusion even more startling and breathtaking. You know exactly what I'm talking about. We've all seen it much too often. I remember hearing a guy rip off a story out of a fairly popular book at the time and put himself in as the principal character. Oh yes, he did! I thought—you have got to be kidding.

My buddy Wayne and I used to do this for fun. We would take illustrations out of Billy Beacham's Student Discipleship curriculum and put ourselves into the story. This was especially amusing to us whenever we were with Billy at some conference or luncheon. I used to love to talk about the time my dad ran a drawbridge for the railroad company – and how one day when I was with him at work, the train was coming and he saw that I was playing down amongst the giant gears that would raise and lower the bridge. He had to make a decision: Crush his son and save the people in the train or vice versa. So I died that day. A bit of silliness, no doubt. Billy would laugh, probably not at us, but certainly near us. Of course, we both thought we were so clever.

But can you believe it when you hear people stand on that hallowed place where we get to teach God's truths to teenagers, put their integrity on the shelf and, as the Chinese proverb says, "paint the snake and add legs"? We had a guy speak at our camp a few years ago, whose stories got so dramatic and almost otherworldly, that our kids started to cast aspersions upon his credibility. They kept asking, "Can that much amazing stuff happen to one guy?" I silently wondered the same thing. They finally stopped listening, because they stopped believing him.

Hey, it's easy to do. If you've ever talked on a regular basis to a group, you know how easy the line is crossed. I've actually caught myself in the act and have learned to correct the exaggeration on the spot. The kids probably don't even notice it, but it makes a difference within my own spirit.

. . .

## Give Credit Where Credit Is Due

One last comment on authenticity in ministry comes in response to the vast epidemic of spiritual plagiarism within ministry circles. It's probably been going on since New Testament days. I can just imagine Philemon pulling his three points out of one of Paul's letters one Saturday night and forgetting to mention that fact the next morning. I honestly think this is usually nothing like the kid who copies and pastes her research paper from Wikipedia the night before it's due. But it is still a problem just the same.

For ten years, from the mid '80s to the mid '90s, Louie Giglio had a Bible study in Waco called Choice. So on most Monday nights during the school year, you would find me sitting amongst a thousand or so Baylor students taking notes like a madman. It was amazing to sit under this man's teaching ministry week after week. One of my associates at the time never missed a Monday night of Choice. Understandably so, this was a huge part of David's life spiritually. But I began to notice that he was quoting Louie liberally during his Wednesday night talks to our junior high group. Sometimes he would give the same talk, dumbed down a lot, but still the same points, same illustrations, everything. The only problem was that he never gave Louie credit for the inspiration and information. When I finally talked to him about it, I realized that he didn't know that he was doing anything wrong. This was such good stuff, and he wanted our kids to hear it. I told him just to mention Louie's name, give credit where credit is due, and continue on with what he was doing. It was a good lesson for him to learn, which he did gladly with results.

To use quotes, illustrations, scriptural insight from others is a no-brainer. Not to give credit is a sin. It will get you an automatic F on an essay. It will expose your integrity as flawed in a talk. I heard about a guest preacher who lifted an outline out of a preaching resource for a Sunday morning, presenting the material as his own. The very next Sunday, the returning pastor preached that same sermon. Ouch! Now that's embarrassing.

I got to hear John Piper speak at a conference where he made an off the cuff remark about Jacob and Esau, talking about how Esau was faced with a dilemma – choose God or choose oatmeal. I wrote an entire talk about that and felt compelled to give written credit to Piper on the outline handout, even though the only thing borrowed was that simple phrase. It is the right thing to do – not like the speakers who plagiarize other communicators and think nothing of it. To lift a talk off of a Ben Stuart podcast and present it as your own would most certainly fall into the abyss of fatal flaws – a spiritual shortcoming that has death written all over it.

Annie Dillard in her book *Pilgrim At Tinker Creek* adds a poignant point to the discussion of church and the ministers who lead. "Week after week, we witness the same miracle: that God, for reasons unfathomable, refrains from blowing our dancing bear act to smithereens."[6] Well played! Authenticity is a beautiful thing to behold. Counterfeit genuineness is abysmal. When you meet someone who is completely comfortable in his or her own skin, you get to spend time with someone who personifies authentic living – and that is always a treat. When you encounter someone who is an impersonator, who seeks the applause above all else, you get to waste precious time with a fraud.

I always tell each of our volunteers: Listen, the students you work with will probably not remember much, if any, of what you say. They will forget most of your brilliant teaching points and well-spoken spiritual insight. But they will remember how you lived, how you embodied a genuine lifestyle that was infused with the reality that is Jesus Christ. They will remember how real you were, and that will make all the difference.

# Chapter Five

# STRENGTH BREEDS STRENGTH

*"I must break you."*
Ivan Drago [the big Russian dude in Rocky IV]

I'm a big baseball fan and I love the Texas Rangers. Now I want to go on public record as saying that one of my all-time favorite Ranger moments has nothing to do with a big win, a walk-off homerun, a no-hitter, or even one of their division or league championships. I've witnessed all of the above, but what happened on a hot August night in 1993 is up there with all the rest. That night, I watched on my television as future Hall of Fame pitcher, Nolan Ryan, plunked Robin Ventura with an inside pitch – and blinked my eyes in disbelief as the 26-year-old Ventura charged the mound where the two decades older Ryan waited with no hint of trepidation whatsoever.

Using a move he said he had used in working with cattle on his ranch, Nolan applied a headlock to his younger, seemingly more virile adversary and proceeded to beat the snot out of him. I leapt to my feet and let out a barbaric yawp as if the Cowboys had just scored a touchdown in the Super Bowl. It was a magical moment when a personal favorite, older and odds on to lose such a matchup, took down the cocky, young buck — who from this point forward would be known, first and foremost, as the guy who got shellacked by Nolan Ryan.

When it comes to sport or tests of strength and stamina, the strongest and the skillful are the ones who are usually successful and most admired by interested observers. Only the strong survive (and win) may be true when it comes to athletics. That's why players and coaches watch films of their upcoming opponents in search of weaknesses they can play upon to ensure victory. It's the idea that for me to be strong, you have to be weak. For me to be successful, you have to be less successful — or even worse. If I'm going to be the man, then I must put you in a headlock and diminish your manhood in quantum bursts of declination.

Robin Ventura is one of only five third basemen in history to hit at least 250 homeruns and win five Gold Gloves. One publication picked him as the best third baseman of the '90s. He played in 1,887 major league games, was a two-time All Star, and even once hit two grand slams in one game. But he will always be most famous for being drilled with a ball and with the fists of a living legend. That beating will be his legacy.


## HA-OOH! HA-OOH! HA-OOH!

It's one thing to celebrate strength and to use it to best your opponent on the playing field, during auditions, or even in a business venture. But is there a place for it in ministry? All too often I see ministers working out of the myth that for my ministry to be strong, your ministry must be weak – or at least weaker. If I am going to be bigger, you must be smaller. If I'm going to have the biggest and best ministry, I must break you. Okay, no one would ever blatantly strategize to beat down the other to make their slice of the pie bigger. Certainly, you would be hard pressed to uncover such a competitive spirit within the pastoral circuit. Surely, we're all in this together – working to build the Kingdom of God, not just our little kingdoms. Yeah, right!

It doesn't take long to realize that the competition between ministries is a constant boil on the butt of vocational integrity. I despise the question, "How big is your youth group?" When someone asks me that, I honestly can't help but think that this person simply wants to see how his or her ministry measures up to mine – to see who is top dog. And I want to ask: Why? What does it matter?

We used to do a city-wide event where several churches would have simultaneous DiscipleNow weekends. We had a common t-shirt and came together on Sunday night for a joint commitment service. It seemed quite fair to divide the cost of the event by the number of students each church had participate. The fellow who had handled the finances was leaving for another church and turned that over to me. When he did so, he informed me that one of the youth pastors in town always called on the following Monday morning to find out how many students each individual church had. I incredulously questioned the possibility of such a thing happening. He simply told me to get ready because the call always came. He was right.

The morning after the event, the aforementioned youth pastor called and asked me to email him the breakdown of numbers for all the churches. I paused and finally said, "Okay," – and proceeded to attach the manifest to an email. Within minutes he was calling, almost in a panic, "I couldn't open the document. Could you send it in a different format?" So I did – it was the only way I could satisfy his out of control longing to see who won. He didn't.

When the competition and the bragging rights become that huge a priority, we get to witness a caricature of ministry in action. All the characteristics are exaggerated, and it's not pretty. That's why I would never let those artists at Six Flags draw a caricature of me. They will most certainly make me look balder, fatter, goofier than I really am. I've got enough problems in the looks department as it is. Why would I want to let some starving artist smear me literally all over a canvas with hilarious exaggerations?

So why do we let the standards of the world dictate the standards on how we do ministry? That's exactly what turns off so many spiritual skeptics. The accusations of spiritual conquest for the sake of numbers hit the fan, as we continue to present this grotesque characterization of the body of Christ. A professor from my days in seminary said it well. The world does not reject Jesus Christ, only the caricature of Christ that we present in our fumbling, bumbling ways. Well played, Dr. Thompson! When the object becomes bigger numbers, cooler facilities, slicker publications, and the most popular leaders, it puts a bigger nose, a weaker chin, a bulging belly, and dumbo-like ears on the body of Christ – and the world is repulsed. Then we find that we are all weaker, not stronger because of it.

The Spartans portrayed in the motion picture *300* would periodically throw back their shoulders and shout at gut-level, "HA-OOH! HA-OOH! HA-OOH!" It was a shout of unity and dedication, and I personally found it very motivating. I'm sure I would have been fired up and ready to take on any gang of Persians that I might bump into in the theater parking lot afterwards. Certainly the story of the 300 is a testament to the strength found when individuals are committed never to letting "We" become "I". This was not a shout of "Look at me!" – even though each of the Spartans in the movie had one of those well-chiseled bodies that I can only dream about. Rather, it was a shout of "We are one! Now bring it on!" On the other hand, to see a youth leader throw back the shoulders and rattle off such an ostentatious boast seems ridiculous to say the least. I've heard it with my own ears.

## The Most Comprehensive Ministry In The City

I read the letter of resignation with great interest. The news was actively churning in the rumor mill, and, sure enough, here was the letter published in the church's monthly newsletter for all to see. This youth minister was actually being terminated by a church that never did such a thing. Therefore, he was mercifully being allowed to resign. I still have brain cells unconsciously devoted to remembering this particular portion of the letter, all these many years later, simply because it was so brazen – especially since it was written by someone who was being sacked. It read, "We have developed the most comprehensive youth ministry in the city. It's not perfect – just the best."

You can imagine how incredulous I was, as I sat there and re-read what I thought I must have misunderstood. But there it was. His "Ha-ooh" was a shout of "I am the greatest – and I'm downright proud of it." I wanted to pick up my phone, call him, and demand that he write another letter – a letter of apology to every youth minister in the city.

How does one go about determining the best, most comprehensive ministry in a city with many such ministries? Was it the one with the biggest numbers? Because that wasn't true. Was it the one with the most activities? Well, that's stupid. Was it the one with the coolest youth minister? Remember, I was doing ministry in this same city, and you can probably already tell, if you're this deep into this book, how cool I am (yeah, right). Honestly, I think if we were able to come up with a sure-fire, bona-fide ability to determine which ministry is best and most comprehensive, it would probably be a dark horse candidate. We're talking, some guy or girl who is loving God and loving kids and making disciples in such an unassuming manner that it might never be noticed and would not be a point of concern, in the least bit, on the part of this youth ministry champion. There would be no "Ha-oohs" coming out of the mouth of this one, only praise given to the Father for all good things.

I never made the phone call, and there was never a letter of apology. Probably, if truth be known, these were not the words of a self-assured, braggadocios conceit, but rather the reflections of a wounded heart with the deep need to justify self and worth. But it doesn't diminish the audacity of the words and the subliminal message of strength and weakness and of winners and losers.

Ronny, a member of our youth staff from a few years back, stood at the fence of a high school girls soccer match and listened as another local youth minister (who was obviously unaware that Ronny was on our staff) tried his best to talk one of our girls into coming to his retreat instead of ours. He was relentless, and Ronny was ticked. It was blatant proselytizing – one trying to grow his ministry at the expense of another. This was while there were tons of kids at that same soccer match who were dying spiritually. All that energy, minus so much integrity, expended to coerce a lamb to move from one flock to another – while the mountainside was teeming with sheep without a shepherd, downcast and distressed and lost.

## This One Thing Is Certain

A principle that has never changed in youth

ministry throughout the years is the simple fact that kids come attached to kids. I don't know of too many students who sat down with a legal pad and listed the pros and cons of the various ministries to decide which one was best for them. In fact, I think that youth ministers everywhere might be a little surprised to find out how little their hip, charismatic leadership had to do with the number of students coming to their stuff. Kids come attached to kids. They usually end up going where their friends go. So it is increasingly important not to take it too personally if one of your students ends up plugged into another ministry.

I've seen youth ministers badger wayward kids senselessly for not coming to their programs. And for what reason? The kid is experiencing community and is part of a discipling journey with another group. So what's wrong with that? It's that personal little kingdom vs. God's Big Kingdom debate all over again. And it just doesn't make sense.

Several years ago, we were the first ones around to pick up some pretty cool video editing equipment to be used at a consumer level. This was way before Apple's iMovie and such. So I offered use of the equipment to other area youth pastors who might want to put together a camp video or something. One day, Paul, from a church just a few miles from us, was in my office editing a video from his recent retreat. At one point, he called me into the room to ask a technical question. As we were looking at the footage, a girl from a family in our church popped up on the screen. Paul later confided that he cringed when he saw Karli's image playing on the raw footage. He thought that I would be upset for sure to see one of ours so prominently displayed at his event.

Now I can be as territorial as the next guy, but on this day, I showed some sporadic maturity and the Kingdom mindset I'm talking about in this chapter. I guess everyone can get lucky once in awhile. I asked, "Was that Karli?" Paul reluctantly responded that it was indeed. Now I don't want to gloat, but I want you to look at my reaction. "That is so cool that she has found a place in your group. We have not been able to get her plugged in here at all." It was true. Later on, young Paul, still in the embryonic stages of discovering God's call on his life, stated that my response had had a profound impact on him. It taught him volumes about ministry and the ministers who lead them.

It wasn't that Karli didn't like me or disapproved of the way we were doing ministry at our church. She was simply attached to some kids at Paul's church, and she discovered a place of community where she could grow in her faith. It worked for her. I was legitimately pleased for her – and that was good.

Hey, sometimes it hurts when someone you loved and poured energy into takes off for "greener pastures" – and quite often it is a revelation of that student's self-indulgent nature, their sense of entitlement. You can't always keep it from hurting your feelings. I have certainly felt my share of sadness from what I thought were hedonistic sons and daughters, abandoning ship without so much as a good-bye or parting gift. That's why we must maintain perspective throughout the ordeal. They almost for certain went to where they were attached – even if they tell you otherwise. Sometimes you have to teach parents this fact as well, especially when they want to ream you out for not keeping their kid involved. Kids come attached to kids. That never has changed, nor will it ever.

## One Plus One Equals More Than Two

Steven Covey's *Seven Habits of Highly Effective People* offers many transferable concepts for ministry. For me, one that stands out is the principle of synergy. He says that synergy simply means "two heads are better than one." The idea is that one plus one can equal two if you want to focus solely on individual effort. But together, in a synergistic environment, we can discover that "the whole is greater than the sum of the parts. One plus one equals three, or six, or sixty."[1] It's a habit where entities come together to cooperate creatively and accomplish so much more than they could have otherwise.

This idea is definitely based on the ability to find

value in our differences – to see that ministries of all kinds bring something to the table. Years ago, I used to play guitar in the band for city-wide Young Life rallies. It was fun because we were playing a lot of Eagles' tunes at the time. But it was also a way to publicly validate the great value that this "para-church" ministry brought to the spiritual life of our city. I've talked with way too many Young Life leaders who wondered why a local youth minister seemed to resent their presence on the campus. It doesn't make sense to me. One day, Michael gushed with me about his excitement over the three "smokers" who attended his Young Life club the previous week. I rejoiced with him, realizing that these were three that my church might not ever get in the door.

I love the word "alchemy". Its meaning is ripe with spiritual possibilities. It's a process of taking ordinary things and turning them into something extraordinary. In Paulo Coelho's *The Alchemist*, an explanation is given to the principal character, Santiago: "The alchemists spent years in their laboratories, observing the fire that purified the metals. They spent so much time close to the fire that gradually they gave up the vanities of the world. They discovered that the purification of the metals had led to a purification of themselves."[2]

To wring out the philosophical leanings of this medieval occupation, to be totally immersed in the process of turning something common into something special, would close the book on the concerns voiced in this chapter. It would mean that we were so close to the refining fire of God's active presence that our vanities would be purged away, and we might not even notice. Instead we would observe with pure eyes and work with clean hands and rejoice in what God, the one and true alchemist, has wrought.

Years ago, I invited a local youth pastor to be a part of a rather large outreach event. We always had so many junior highs come to this annual affair that we welcomed, with open arms, any and all youth workers from other churches or ministries. He came and I was glad to have him. But the next year we noticed that the same event was down numerically by a significant number from the previous year. I especially felt the drop in attendance in the financial area, as we lost right at a thousand bucks that night. Understand that this was an autumn tradition that was fifteen years old and had always paid for itself. It wasn't until a few weeks later that I found out that my invited guest had duplicated the exact same event under a different name two weeks before ours. Not two weeks after, not in the spring – but just days before ours.

As diplomatically as possible, I asked him about it over coffee. He saw no problem with it – wouldn't budge, wouldn't consider another part of the year. Since it was a middle school activity, it only took two years to complete the heist. We soon were splitting the numbers down the middle, causing me to adjust our approach and to apply budget dollars to fund the evening. Why would he do this? In my humble opinion, he wanted to "break me." Arguably, but not really, he wanted to win – to get a bigger, make that the biggest, slice of the pie.

This is not about numbers, really. It is about synergy, about alchemy – about the whole of the Kingdom being increased and something divinely special happening in the process. It is about realizing that strength breeds strength. It's adopting the mindset that for us to be stronger, then we desire others to be stronger. A stronger presence of Christ in your community can enhance the opportunity that there might be a stronger presence of Christ in your individual ministry. Jeremiah 9:23-24 encapsulates it perfectly, *"Let no wise man boast of his wisdom, nor let the mighty man boast of his might, nor a rich man boast of his riches; but let the one who boasts boast of this, that he understands and knows Me, that I am the Lord who exercises mercy, justice, and righteousness on the earth; for I delight in these things," declares the Lord."*[3] I can't add anything to that!

# Chapter Six

# THE ONE AND ONLY MISSION STATEMENT

*"Here is the test to find whether your mission on earth is finished: If you're alive, it isn't."*
Richard Bach

My first encounter with the concept of a mission statement was when I read Stephen Covey's *Seven Habits of Highly Effective People* – a very pedantic, yet quite descriptive title, and a tremendously insightful read for sure. In the book, the second habit is "Begin with the End in Mind," in which Covey encourages his readers to set a personal mission statement. Just like Barney the dinosaur, he placed strong emphasis on using one's imagination, but not for the purpose of visualizing lemon drops and gumdrops. It's "the ability to envision in your mind what you cannot at present see with your eyes."[1] His idea was that everything is created twice. You have a mental creation, followed by a physical creation – like the blueprint that precedes the actual building. Covey espoused, "Begin with the End in Mind means to begin each day, task, or project with a clear vision of your desired direction and destination, and then continue by flexing your proactive muscles to make things happen."[2]

Of course, everyone in the evangelical world of vocational ministry knows that Rick Warren baptized the concept when he hammered home the ideology of ministry being driven by a purpose. Doug Fields narrowed the focus for youth workers even more in *Purpose Driven Youth Ministry*, whereupon we all immediately penned a mission statement – most of us basically taking Doug's Saddleback example and trying to make it sound originally our own. Instead of using Doug's concentric circles, I gave it a shot using concentric triangles, but finally gave up and went with the circles too – and yes, I gave him credit!

No doubt, this is all really good stuff. It's been said a million times: if you aim at nothing, you'll hit it every time. All three of the previously mentioned books had a profound impact on me, resulting in paradigm shifts in my ministry approach that were needed and residually effective. One thing is for sure, I don't need to write a chapter on this subject, because how could you ever top these guys? Not gonna happen.

So what is the point of this chapter? Good question. Let's just suffice it to say, that I want everyone in youth ministry, from those with mission statement already in daily operation to those who are clueless as to what even tomorrow holds, to make sure that it all lines up with the one and only mission statement. Jesus laid out purpose-driven ministry with the Great Commission: *Go therefore and make disciples of all the nations, baptizing them in the name of the Father and of the Son and of the Holy Spirit, teaching them to observe all that I have commanded you. And behold, I am with you always, to the end of the age.*[3]

I know the Great Commission is all over the Purpose-Driven course of action. I understand that fully. It's just that I continue to be amazed at how many youth ministries seem to be totally missing what I believe is the point of Matthew 28:19-20: Evangelizing and discipling. Go and tell, then disciple. Isn't that what Jesus is saying? Now in an earlier chapter, I've already confessed as to what a theological lightweight I am. So I'm not going to try to impress you with my exegetical skills. But I do want to clear off a space and throw a fit about how important balance is in this area. It's so simple, yet so profound. It's so easily understood, yet so easily ignored. You have to admit that Jesus did not stutter here as He articulated the perfect mission statement.

. . .

## Give Me The Gas

When I go to the dentist for the serious stuff... you know fillings and root canals and such...I always request the gas. Of course, I'm talking about nitrous oxide or, as it is affectionately called, laughing gas. Why the gas? Hey, it replaces pain with a euphoric, pleasurable sensation, leaving you in such a state as to allow the dentist to do whatever he or she pleases with your teeth, roots, and nerve endings. Pump a little Pink Floyd or Steely Dan through the head-phones and I'm thinking, "Go ahead and rotate my teeth while you're in there." Since part of my life's creedal path has always included the statement, "No pain, no pain," why would I not insist on the gas?

It's hard for me to understand my parents' genera-tion. My mom would have surgery and be proud that she was not using her pain medication. I'm thinking, "How much longer until I can take my next pill?" I've actually only been put to sleep via general anesthesia once. That was when I had my colonoscopy, and my doctor went where no man has gone before. But I remember lying on my side, looking at the television monitor and wondering where the little camera was. The next thing I know, my wife Debbie is patting me on the arm to awaken me. Weird sensation to be out of it to that degree.

I read this somewhere many years ago, and I wish

I could credit the source, but it goes something like this: "Activity is the anesthetic to deaden the pain of an empty ministry." I read that and never forgot it. Wow! The mission is simply not activity for the sake of activity. It is much more than that. Filling a calendar to impress your pastor and your parents might make an impression on the aforementioned, but it is not the answer to breathing life into your ministry. Sure you are busy, but busy doing what? If you get in your car and start driving with no intended destination in mind (like a drive in the country), you may enjoy the scenery and have a pleasant conversation with your passengers, but you never arrive anywhere but back where you started.

To anesthetize oneself with purposeless activities may fallaciously convince others of what a good job you're doing. But when you wake up and wonder what happened, when the "medication" starts to wear off, when you're suddenly aware of the reality that surrounds you, then you know deep, deep inside that it's not decent at all. The ever present emptiness starts to creep back in. An empty, directionless ministry will always leave you with a void that threatens to crater at any moment.

A colleague of mind introduced me to the concept of "programming with a purpose" way back in the mid '80s. This was before Covey, Warren, and Fields perfected the idea in later years. It immediately made sense to me. I started to examine the purpose behind every event, every program. As we culled the fluff away, the focus became so much clearer. Doug Fields said, "I would estimate that less than ten percent of the student ministries I have seen, talked to, or consulted have been able to articulate their reason for existence. Even fewer have communicated it with a clear mission statement for others to embrace and follow."[4]

A former student, who was then in his first part-time youth ministry position, called me one day. After the initial chitchat, he got down to crux of the matter. "I'm sitting in my office, and I don't know what to do." I asked him what he meant. He reiterated, "I don't know what to do... next." He literally was sitting there clueless as to how he should spend his time in ministry that afternoon. There was no doubt that he wanted to be used, just not sure how. This is a guy who is doing extremely effective ministry presently at a church in Dallas. But at that moment, he was miserably spinning his wheels in ministerial oblivion. At least he had the guts to be honest about it.

Well the one thing I didn't tell him to do was go plan some more activities. That wasn't the answer. In fact, I don't really remember exactly what I told him, but I bet it had a lot of references to the Great ComMission statement. Now I could have shared this quote from Thomas Merton (if I had known about it way back when.) This would have been real good.

> "When our activity is habitually disordered, our malformed conscience can think of nothing better to tell us than to multiply the quantity of our acts, without perfecting their quality. And we go from bad to worse, exhaust ourselves, empty our whole life of all content, and fall into despair...[sometimes] we simply have to sit back for a while and do nothing."[5]

Hey, I remember now that I told him to sit back for a while and do nothing (or something to that extent)—and figure out what he needed to do to accomplish the goals of reaching new students, and then teaching them how to consistently follow Jesus.

## My Food Is To Be Involved In Successful Ministry

In John 4, the disciples urge Jesus to eat (right after His encounter with the woman at the well). He responds, *"I have food to eat that you do not know about."* While they were wondering who brought take out to Jesus, He comes out with a classic, *"My food is to do the will of Him who sent Me and to accomplish His work."*[6] I had been in ministry for over twenty years before I began to better understand what Jesus was talking about. It happened at a border crossing into Morocco.

I had a group of high school students on mission trip. Our main task was to hand out Campus Crusades' *Jesus* videos and translated New Testaments at the border to Moroccans who did not want them. We did this for several hours a day, walking up to waiting cars or alongside of those on foot with a smile and a "free gift". Needless to say, very few packets were received. I did see one man receive the packet and then, intentionally in our line of vision, vigorously slam dunk it in a trash can. But most would pass us by as if we were tambourine-thumping Hare Krishnas. Many would wave their finger at us as to say, "No, no, no...I know exactly what you're up to." After a steady diet of apathy and after receiving the proverbial finger of rejection countless times, I began to despise what I was doing and felt my heart shrinking dispassionately for these who dwelt in such spiritual darkness.

It just so happened that I stumbled upon this passage during our overseas stay, and I saw it through a much different lens for the first time. I had one of those epiphanies that came straight from God. It was the realization that my food had always been to do the will of the Father – that is as long as it meant successful ministry. I couldn't stomach ministry that seemed pointless and offered not even a slight glimmer of possible success. This was a good teaching moment for me and provided a much better perspective on what ministry is all about. Having everything you touch turn to gold was nice, but not the point.

To do the will of the Father and to be a part of accomplishing His work means to follow in the steps of Jesus. Those steps take us to a place where we realize that the Father desires all "to be saved and to come to a knowledge of the truth." Succinctly put for me, that boils down ministry-wise to a simple formula: Do the right thing. Do it consistently. Do it with excellence. To see kids come to Christ and become devoted to following Him daily means staying focused on that very simple target.

## Do The Right Thing. Do It Consistently. Do It With Excellence.

I was a youth pastor at a church in the Fort Worth area during the early '80s for almost six years. During that time, I went to the local middle school and high school every week during the lunch period. The schools allowed that – so I took advantage of the opportunity to "constructively hang around" during the two lunch periods. I met tons of kids and saw many come into our ministry due, in part, to this weekly touch. It was the right thing to do, and I was extremely consistent in having that campus presence. I wasn't the coolest or most hilarious person hanging around the school, just the most consistent.

The high school had a baccalaureate service for its senior class every May. For years, the local ministerial association had picked the speaker for this service, which meant it was passed around amongst the various pastors of the more predominant churches. The last year I was there, they made a change. It was decided that the senior class of 350 students would vote on a baccalaureate speaker. I guess you can figure out where this is headed. I was picked as the speaker – not because I was such a great orator, which I'm not, and not because I was wildly popular and charismatic, which I'm not, and not even because of my good looks – but because of my consistency. I had been with those kids from seventh grade through their senior year, and they recognized that.

I can't begin to tell you how many times I would walk away from the campus, thinking, "What did I just accomplish besides wasting away two hours of an already full day?" Often that sense of futility would thrust me into questioning the validity of such activity. But I knew inside that it was the right thing to do – so I continued to press on: hanging around the cafeteria, attending all kinds of athletic events, choir concerts, plays, even debate tournaments.

As an aside, I must share a little tactic that I referred to in chapter three and that continues to serve me well. If you plan right, you can arrive at a choir or band concert towards the end, hear the last song or two, and then just hang around the foyer afterwards. If you're very careful with your wording – "Wow, that last song was really terrific!" – you can get full credit from students and parents for being at the event. Also, if you go to a sporting event, make sure you take one long, slow stroll in front of the home bleachers. Most everyone will see you. I don't think this is being deceitful. I call it being a good steward of your time. Whatever you call it, it works.

Back to the point: the right thing is to stay committed to bringing new students to Christ. This continues to become more and more difficult as we live in these complex, sophisticated times. To settle into a holy huddle is to miss the point of Christ's commission. To accomplish that is to keep working and tweaking and exploring until you hit on the means to that end. Currently in our ministry, we find it interesting that our small groups are reaching as many new students as our midweek outreach event. It would seem that the deep need for community, that which a small group affords, is drawing new faces into the fold. Whatever it takes!

Excellence...let me talk to you for a moment about excellence. This is where too many ministries fall short. It's hard to keep up a high standard of programming week after week. I know sometimes, after a week of camp or a mission trip where you have poured yourself out spiritually, physically, and emotionally, I find myself sitting at my desk on Monday and looking square in the face of another round of regular weekly activities. It's like the mail. It never stops. It's the reason why we have the term "go postal" as a part of our cultural slang and everyone knows exactly what it means. Now the ministry version of "going postal" doesn't involve automatic weapons. It involves the devaluing of excellence as a core value. It's called mailing it in, creatively and spiritually, and settling for something banal and hopelessly mediocre.

The Turner Prize (a prestigious award given for achieving excellence in the area of visual arts) was given to an artist in 2001 for his work entitled, "The lights going on and off." The award-winning artwork consisted of a simple room that had lights that intermittently turned on and off, over and over again. And that was it. Another artist, outraged by the award, threw eggs against the walls of the room, which prompted an interested observer to muse what a waste of eggs that was. Other protesters, who were not thrilled about public money being used for such an inane exhibit, organized a picket line, complete with flashlights that they carried, and intermittently turned on and off, over and over again.

To take shortcuts in the area of creative excellence is a seductive avenue that pulls many away from the right course. When we start googling at the last minute for a mixer, while we pull an old talk out of the file, as we scramble through YouTube in search of anything to show, we are taking shortcuts that will leave us flipping the lights on and off, just hoping the kids will think it's cool enough. Guess what? Here's the good news/bad news. The good news is that they will not organize a protest against your pedantic efforts at effective programming. There will be no picket lines or vandalism. The bad news is you'll eventually end up with a room full of empty chairs – and you'll be making a huge deposit in the growing bank account of indifference.

To be excellent requires commitment over the long haul. It means never settling for the ordinary when the extraordinary can be attained through a tenacious attitude. Aristotle put it well, "We are what we repeatedly do. Excellence, then, is not an act, but a habit." Adopting the habit of excellence as a part of the process will make what you do more effective and provide a sense of spiritual fulfillment along the way. Creative elements are always the first thing to go. Then we chunk thorough study in preparation for teaching times. What that leaves is fill-in-the-blanks programs that are google-driven and perfunctory. This is ministry that totally lacks staying power.

### Make Yourselves At Home In My Love

The Message's re-wording of John 15 has Jesus saying, *"I've loved you the way my Father has loved me. Make yourselves at home in My love. If you keep my commands, you'll remain intimately at home in my love.*

*That's what I've done—kept my Father's commands and made myself at home in his love."[7]* This He spoke in the upper room to His disciples – His small group. To do the right thing in youth ministry includes a total devotion to this disciple-making process. We must put kids in a place where they can make themselves at home in the love of the Father.

One thing I discovered many years ago is the fact that I can't disciple every kid. I can't be the spiritual mentor to all these that I love. I tried. I failed. To enlist and empower adults to pour themselves into the lives of students is of the greatest necessity. To have a strategy that enables the process of mentoring to take place can represent a lifetime of change.

I have the distinct advantage and privilege of working within fifteen minutes of the largest Baptist university in the world. Therefore, I have around thirty college students who work as volunteers in our small group ministry. Every fall as we prepare for another year, I tell them this simple truth: Discipleship is more caught than taught—that the kids they work with will not remember so much what they say, as much as how they lived. Because of that, we try to strategize so that the leader/small group relationship becomes a multi-year affair. I have actually had Baylor students work with, basically, the same group for all four years of their university career. To top that, Kayleigh (who actually went through our ministry as a middle school and high school student) stayed on with her small group all the way through her master's degree - working with them from seventh grade through high school graduation. I actually performed Kayleigh's wedding during that last year and got a little emotional as I watched her small group being escorted in as her house party. By the way, that small group of five seventh graders was up to nineteen on the day of her wedding (trying to split up high school girls is worse than trying to split a senior adult Sunday School class).

I consider our small group ministry as the real heartbeat of our program. Still, I am amazed at how many youth ministries make no real tangible efforts in this area. To be dedicated to this process requires enlisting and nurturing volunteers, having a well thought out scope and sequence to the content, and motivating kids to buy into the idea. One cool by-product for us has been that the majority of our leaders, like Kayleigh, are former students. They have totally bought into the legitimacy of this ministry and want to turn around and give right back to it. Another of the by-products is the life-long relationships that are being established. Many of these mentoring relationships will last long after they have forgotten the name of their old youth pastor. And that's good. It's the right thing to do – a non-negotiable. Not to have this as a huge, viable part of a youth ministry is to have a ministry that is rootless and toothless, and probably of little consequence in the grand scheme of God's kingdom.

Jesus goes on in John chapter fifteen, *"I've named you friends because I've let you in on everything I've heard from the Father."* I love that...let you in on everything I've heard from the Father. It's such a transferable concept – the opportunity to let kids in on the good things we have learned from the Father. What a beautiful and simple way to describe the discipleship process. He goes on to call us to bear fruit that won't spoil. That's another good way to re-phrase the Great Commission. Bear fruit and do what it takes to keep that fruit from spoiling. It's a noble call from the Father, through Jesus, directly to the heart of ministry. Anything less than that would be adequate but not very good. Who wants to settle for that?

# Chapter Seven

## WHAT GOES UP, MUST COME DOWN

*What goes up must come down,*
*Spinning wheel got to go round*
*Talking about your troubles it's a crying sin*
*Ride a painted pony, let the spinning wheel spin*
Blood, Sweat, and Tears 1969

Probably about once every couple of years or so, I spend two or three days contemplating a sudden move from ministry, thinking it's time to get the heck out of Dodge (or, in my case, Waco). The only other career that even sounds remotely interesting is being a sports reporter, hanging out in the Dallas Cowboy locker room collecting player interviews. Not gonna happen. But I can sink into that stream of conscious-ness because our attendance was down one time, even though it was way high the week before. Waylaid by a row of empty chairs or a couple of sophomore guys who seem disinterested in my talk, I make my way home and begin contemplating how one goes about breaking into sports journalism. Should I go back to school? Who do I know that could help me get a foot in the door? If I get to do sideline reporting on television, how will I avoid being featured on YouTube, making a fool of myself? Should I shave off my goatee? The thought process gets more and more weird.

It's amazing how one round of supposed difficulty can take you to the depths of possible career suicide. In some strange way, I'm glad this happens occasionally. If for no other reason, the lows eventually bring me back to the realization of how blessed I am to get to spend my life working with kids. Tim Hansel in his encouraging work, *You Gotta Keep Dancing*, reasons that your cup of joy can only be as deep as your cup of sorrow.[1] I had to chew on that for awhile to fully comprehend where he was headed. I figured that it meant when you experience a low, you are better able to grasp and fully enjoy the joy that comes from the high.

In the classic flick, *Parenthood*, Steve Martin's character Gil plays the father who put the hyphen in anal-retentive. He is so tightly wound up in his complicated life that he is on the verge of ruining his family in the process. During one scene, Grandma saunters into the room as Gil bemoans his sad state of affairs and randomly begins talking about when Grandpa took her on a roller coaster when she was nineteen. Gil is a little put off with the sudden change of subject, but Grandma is very animated about the ride. "Up, down, up, down." His sarcasm is thick in acknowledging her "great story." But then Grandma brings it home, "I always wanted to go again. You know, it was just so interesting to me that a ride could make me so frightened, so scared, so sick, so excited, and so thrilled all together! Some didn't like it. They went on the merry-go-round. That just goes around. Nothing. I like the roller coaster. You get more out of it."[2]

Thanks, Grandma, for a ton of beautiful perspective. Later on in the movie, the family is at the all too familiar school play when Gil's little one begins to wreak havoc on the stage. Gil's initial reaction is to race up and put things back in their proper order. But then Grandma's words come to metaphorical life, as he chooses to sit down and, for once, enjoy the ride. The seats in the theater suddenly take on the life of a roller coaster and their inhabitants become riders, coasting up and down. Laughter and pure enjoyment spill over the room, and Gil's face reflects all of this and more.

So frightened, so scared, so sick, so excited, and so thrilled all together! You gotta like the roller coaster! What goes up, must come down. What comes down, must go up! That's almost always true. If you get out at the bottom, you, most assuredly, get out of having to make the climb back to the top. You also miss the best part that is soon to come. There is a ride at Six Flags Over Texas called the Titan. It is not for the faint of heart. This one goes very high and falls just as quickly. There's a part of the ride where I can sometimes feel on the verge of blacking out. It's a strange sensation to experience and probably not good for someone who takes a little pill every morning to keep that blood pressure in check. But the free fall is unbelievable! And so worth it!

What goes up, must come down. Just like the Dow Jones, as we all fully know, this principle is inevitable. The unknown factor is what we will do during the down times.

## It's Better To Burn Out Than To Fade Away

I really don't feel like I have ever come anywhere close to burn out. I've had lots of friends and acquaintances who have claimed to be burnt out. And I have to admit that some of these looked the part of how you would imagine a burn out victim would appear. Now I've been pretty down before – really feeling sorry for myself. When it's late and you're scraping Skittles or candle wax out of the carpet because you can't afford to get the building mainte-nance guy mad at you (knowing full well that he thinks he is third in charge, just behind the pastor and the pastor's administrative assistant – and he has ways of making your life miserable), a nice, tidy eight to five job starts to look attractive. But that's about as far as I've ever gotten. That seems far, far away from burn out.

Nirvana's Kurt Cobain quoted a Neil Young song in his suicide note in 1994. "It's better to burn out, than to fade away."[3] There's that burn out phrase again. Actually, Neil Young wrote the lyric in response to the punk movement that was starting up in the late '70s–that was making him feel irrelevant, kind of a rock and roll dinosaur. Now I can relate to that for sure. To be this old in youth ministry can play on your mind – leading to fears of fading away and no longer being relevant nor significant – and I guess, in some instances, teetering on the edge of burn out. Cobain's letter goes on to cry out, "I'm too sensitive. I need to be slightly numb in order to regain the enthusiasms I once had as a child." He mulls over how his daughter reminds him of how he used to be, loving and trusting of all. This guy was definitely burnt out – and it cost him dearly.

NYC psychologist, Herbert Freudenberger, is credited with coming up with the term "burn out" and defines it as an emotional state where one is overwhelmed by feelings of exhaustion, coupled with aggravation. It would seem that it is a condition in which a person's creativity and ability to stay effective begin to wear down, leaving them fatigued and cynical. Of course, the ability to function effectively goes out the door. Neil Young's 1979 song where the "fade away" quote was lifted was actually titled "Hey, Hey, My, My (Into the Black)" – and was supposedly a reference to a phrase coined by soldiers who were a part of that little so-called police action occurring in Vietnam in the '60s and '70s. "Out of the blue and into the black" was very descriptive of the act of leaping from daylight into the blackness of a Vietcong tunnel. Leaving light and life and falling into darkness and the absolute possibility of death certainly serves as a severe analogy for burn out. To be exhausted physically, emotionally, and spiritually leaves one vulnerable and desperate, with a sense of falling into a black hole where escape is not even an option.

I think the reference to the loss of creativity makes for an interesting aspect regarding the debilitating lows that accompany possible burn out. Is this where we begin to lose our ability to be creative? It was unbelievably insightful of the Canadian poet, Michael St. George, when he was asked when he became a poet. His response, "When did most of us stop being poets? Kids are just natural artists – they sing, dance, make up poems...Everyone is basically creative."[4] Then somewhere along the way, we lose it. What is it about children and their propensity to be creative? Even Kurt Cobain seemed mesmerized by the innocence and non-existent inhibitions of his young daughter.

One evening, my daughter Hannah, then four years old, stood on her chair at a restaurant and begin singing "Rudolph, The Red-Nose Reindeer". There was a dozen or so youth workers with my wife and me that night and no one had noticed her performance had begun. "Excuse me! Excuse me!" she exclaimed loudly until she had everybody's complete and undivided attention. Then she proceeded to give a rousing rendition of this Christmas classic, start to finish – and then, quite obviously, thoroughly enjoyed the ovation she received as she put the finishing touches on the song.

No doubt, she served as a representation of the poet in all of us – no sign of inhibition, imagination spilling over into her small world, not willing to be side-tracked by perceived indifference. Something happens to most of us as we grow up. We stop being poets. That reservoir of creativity starts to dry up and threatens to disappear completely. In the beautifully made movie, *Finding Neverland*, Johnny Depp's character of J.M. Barrie secures twenty-five seats at the premiere of *Peter Pan* and places children from a local orphanage in them. His idea is brilliant, because it's the laughter and innocent charm of the children that primes the pump in the theater that night – enabling a bunch of stuffy adults to re-discover those child-like qualities within themselves. And a good time was had by all.

I had a moment like that a few years back. At lunch one day at my daughter's school, it happened. The lunchroom monitor was offering a blessing over the meal. As she was drawing the prayer to a close, she concluded, "Bless this food to the nourishment of our bottoms." Of course, the room was filled with the giggles of children who were delighted at such a faux pas. I must admit that I was among the gigglers, trying desperately to suppress the laughter that was sure to come. When she managed to finally mutter an amen, the whole room broke out in unabashed laughter – and even though I tried to maintain some sense of decorum I found myself joining right in. It felt somewhat immature to be laughing with school children about the idea of a booty blessing – and it was. But you have to admit, that's pretty funny.

With society pressing against us and stress mounting up its steady assault on our psyches, creativity can quickly become a casualty in the pursuit of effective ministry. A child is not easily deterred in creative pursuits. Given a sheet a paper and some markers, a kid sees nothing but a green light to the fast lane of self-expression. Having the tools of artistry shoved off the table and replaced with an overstuffed inbox of demands, complaints, and absurd requests can easily kill off any remaining imagination cells in any resident adult. Then one can find themselves burning out and fading away.


## You Know You're Having A Bad Day...

...When you call the suicide prevention hotline and they put you on hold. I bet that happened to the poor guy at Decca Records, who supposedly rejected the Beatles after their audition in 1962. He is credited with this now famous quote, "We don't like their sound, and guitar music is on the way out." I wonder if that guy ever recovered from that colossal misevaluation of talent and the music culture that was to be. Now that's what I call a bad day. As he watched the meteoric rise of the Fab Four and the ensuing avalanche of record sales, I can just imagine that the low kept getting lower. Sometimes you just miss the mark. Bad days are inevitable. How you handle them will make all the difference.

I listened to a talk by Bill Hybels on a cassette many, many years ago where he talked about spiritual skimming. It happens when you allow the draining relationships to outnumber the replenishing relationships in one's life – and you find yourself emotionally depleted. It made great sense to me. When you're totally spent emotionally, you start skimming out of a need for survival. And emptiness ensues. And isolation. And vulnerability. And finally a desperate need to feel good inside...and to feel good now! It was suggested that the rising number of moral failures in ministry are the result of this emptiness that has been induced by being depleted emotionally, and thus spiritually dry. Loneliness, isolation, discouragement, even depression begin taking its toil as you struggle to get out of the valley.

C.S. Lewis has Wormwood corresponding with his nephew about this very subject in *Screwtape Letters*. He calls it "the state of undulation" – a series of valleys and peaks, rising and falling:

> "If you had watched your patient carefully you would have seen this undulation in every department of his life—his interest in his work, his affection for his friends, his physical appetites, all go up and down. As long as he lives on earth periods of emotional and bodily richness and liveliness will alternate with periods of numbness and poverty. The dryness and dullness through which your patient is now going are not, as you fondly suppose, your workmanship; they are merely a natural phenomenon which will do us no good unless you make a good use of it."[5]

That's a good strategy if you're a demon at work on one of your Christian clients. It really seems to be working these days, using the valleys, the down times to create creatures of self-absorption.

I lived in Puerto Rico for half of my teenage years

(my dad was in the Air Force), and, obviously, we spent a great deal of time at the beach. One of the most memorable was the beach at Rincon. They've actually had the World Surfing Championships at Rincon, which was just minutes from my house. In other words, big waves! I remember boogie boarding and getting toppled over by humongous Caribbean waves – and I remember being thrust down in the water and not knowing for a split second exactly which direction to swim to reach the surface. Weird feeling, not knowing if you'll ever reach the place where oxygen abounds!

I guess it's one reason why I love the ocean. It's so mysterious and dangerous and thrilling and uncertain. It's definitely a good, real life example of undulation – the rising and falling of day-to-day living, the uncertainty of life's unexpected twists mixed with expectations of new adventures. Riding the crest of the wave will not happen unless you struggle back out. If you've ever surfed, you know that you spend a lot more time struggling to get back out than you do riding back in. But is it ever worth it – waves of such size and magnitude, rolling and controlling and taking you to new, exciting, frightening places. I love the way The Message words this passage from Ephesians, *"And I ask him that with both feet planted firmly on love, you'll be able to take in with all Christians the extravagant dimensions of Christ's love. Reach out and experience the breadth! Test its length! Plumb the depths! Rise to the heights!"*[6]

There is a wave of God's presence. We are encouraged to "reach out and experience the breadth! Test its length! Plumb the depths! Rise to the heights!" Leonard Sweet says we have three choices: Catch it, hunker down, or try to ignore it.[7] But one thing is for sure, we do have to make a choice.

It's kind of like spiritual white water rafting. If we choose to go for it, we have our Heavenly Father who, like a much needed guide, takes us through the white water canyon, with a steady, calm hand in the midst of the churning, potentially crunching water. Rapids, that could take your life, give you the ride of a lifetime. Our choice is to stand on the bank and be a wondering spectator – wondering if you could do it and possibly never knowing. Or we can get in the raft and trust the One who guides.

Wormwood continues:

"Now it may surprise you to learn that in His efforts to get permanent possession of a soul, He relies on the troughs even more than on the peaks; some of His special favourites have gone through longer and deeper troughs than anyone else. The reason is this. To us a human is primarily good; our aim is the absorption of its will into ours, the increase of our own area of self-hood at its expense. But the obedience which the Enemy demands of men is quite a different thing...He really does want to fill the universe with a lot of loathsome little replicas of Himself-creatures, whose life, on its miniature scale, will be qualitatively like His own, not because He has absorbed them but because their wills freely conform to His. We want cattle who can finally become food; He wants servants who can finally become sons. We want to suck in, He wants to give out. We are empty and would be filled; He is full and flows over."[8]

Wow! Two different results from the same valley. Interesting proposition, and I guess it's our choice every time.

## Do Something That Scares You

This is absolutely the truth. San Jose State University sponsors a contest where contestants are asked "to compose the opening sentence to the worst of all possible novels." Here's one of the winners:

Delores breezed along the surface of her life like a flat stone forever skipping along smooth water, rippling reality sporadically but oblivious to it consistently, until she finally lost momentum, sank, and due to an overdose of fluoride as a child which caused her to suffer from chronic apathy, doomed herself to lie forever on the floor of her

life as useless as an appendix and as lonely as
a five-hundred pound barbell in a steroid-free
fitness center.[9]

Delores is another example of someone who is
looking for the easy way, just skimming, skipping
along the smooth surface of her life, and thinking she
could do so forever. Then suddenly she sinks like
Leonardo DiCaprio in *Titanic* (my favorite part of
that movie). Everyone wants a life that counts for
something. To lie forever on the floor of life as
useless as an appendix just doesn't seem to cut it for
most people. To be as lonely as a five-hundred pound
barbell in a steroid-free fitness center isn't the life
goal of too many people. But it is exactly where she
doomed herself to be. Her choice totally. There is a
path that leads to greatness, to purpose, to meaning –
but it is a path that is fraught with difficulty, with the
distinct possibility of being another casualty.

The Lord says in Psalm 12, *"I will place him in the
safety for which he longs."*[10] There is safety in God's
faithful hands – meaning there is uncertainty mixed
with assurance, danger mixed with confidence, an
obscure, hidden path mixed with continual signs
giving clear direction – it's called living dangerously,
yet safely in God's faithful hands. (Thank you Steve
Camp.) We are always busy looking for the path of
least resistance. But really, shouldn't we be more

interested in the path of most resistance, because it's not easy – although it is easy when you consider the provision that comes from God for your journey. The hardest, easiest thing you could ever do – or not do. We all have that choice every day.

Author Paulo Coelho puts it very well when he says, "A fall from the third floor hurts as much as a fall from the hundredth. If I have to fall, may it be from a high place."[11] If what goes up must come down, then so it goes. But it will always be worth it to keep going for the high place. "Taking a new step, uttering a new word, is what people fear most,"[12] declares Fyodor Dostoyevsky. It might involve doing something that scares you. We should all do that regularly. Anne Lamott takes us another direction, "When you need to make a decision, and you don't know what to do, just do one thing or the other, because the worst that can happen is that you will make a terrible mistake."[13] Hilarious, yet remarkably true. I like to call it "going for broke," gambling with all your chips. Too many never "go for broke." They end up with a nicely stacked set of chips (the ones they started with). Everything is orderly, the reds and the blues are stacked in separate piles. It is such a safe way to live. Wringing the poker analogy dry, these are the ones who never experience the emotion of raising the ante on life, pushing the stack out there, not knowing the outcome.

Texas Troubadour, Guy Clark wrote a song entitled *The Cape* that captures the essence of risk taking in all stages of life. I encourage you pull it up and give a listen. The song starts with the story of an eight-year-old kid who ties a flour sack cape around his neck and then proceeds to jump off of the garage, with every intention of flying like Superman. Of course, he crashes to the ground. Then comes the young man with dreams and a do-it-or-die attitude who "was pretty sure he could fly" too. The song concludes with the old, grey guy with his cape, still jumping off the garage—with this killer line, "He did not know he could not fly and so he did."[14] The song strongly suggests that all of life is just a leap of faith. So you might as well "spread your arms and hold your breath" and trust that cape.

I always hope that last verse will be the way people see me – old and gray and still jumping off that garage, until the very end. Of course, the end could come sooner than later if I keep jumping off garages. But who wants to fade away...or burn out? And by the way, it's really not about capes. It's about taking the risk, making the difficult climb first, and then spreading those arms and taking that flying leap – and totally trusting that God is there to catch you. He will be.

# Chapter Eight

# ONCE UPON A TIME

*"Either our lives become stories
or there's no way to get through them."*
Douglas Coupland, *Generation X*

"Am I self-centered or is it just me?" That's a funny expression for a button or a t-shirt, just as long as it isn't true for the one displaying such an audacious emblem. Too often, it borders on the truth for many of us. Did you ever, while growing up, wonder, seriously consider it a possibility, that the whole world was a huge movie set and that you were the star? That all the people around you, family, friends, acquaintances, even strangers were just the co-stars and extras in your lifetime cinema directed by God Himself? Talking about a boisterous burp of self-centeredness. Maybe you didn't. I did. Obviously others have had the same thought – like whoever the dude was who wrote the screenplay for *The Truman Show*. I guarantee, he had those same feelings. In the movie, a god-like character served as basically the 'divine director' of a reality television show, calling out camera shots and setting up the next scene for the main character (and the only one not in on the secret). Every once in awhile, there would be a person on the street sneaking a peek in Truman's general direction – and their slight smile would almost give away the whole gigantic secret. It was a perfect world where everything revolved around him. The ongoing storyline entertained millions as they sat glued to their television sets. It was a story you couldn't have made up. It was truth that was stranger, and more entertaining, than fiction.

On a regular basis, when the mood hits me, I will entertain van loads of kids by calling into talk radio stations. It happened the first time while I was leading a procession of vans back home from a mission trip to New Orleans. It was an early Saturday morning and most in my van were fast asleep. Because I didn't feel like it would be a good idea for me to join with them in the nap, I turned on the radio and discovered a call-in radio program out of Baton Rouge about home and gardening. Not sure why, I had never done it before, but I picked up my cell phone and dialed the number they kept repeating over the airwaves. I got through! Wow! I got excited as I talked to the screener and was put on hold. By this time, kids in my van were picking up on what was happening and began waking the others up. Phone calls were made to the other vans to dial in the station on their radios. And for about ten minutes, I entertained our group with a lively, on-air discussion with a fellow who was completely passionate about dirt and grass. I made it up as we were going along, and the suppressed laughter broke out uproariously as soon as I hung up.

We spent the rest of the morning calling into radio programs we found as we tallied up more and more miles of interstate. Since then, I have talked to home improvement programs, (about how my teenage son drove his car through the front wall of my living room), automotive shows (about my teenage son putting regular gas in my diesel truck), and all sorts of investment and sports programs. It always works out well for both parties. Our kids get the biggest kick out of it, and the talk show hosts go crazy with the vivid stories I make up. I don't even have a son. It certainly makes you continue to wonder about some of the stories you hear on reality programming, doesn't it?

Telling stories, truthful or not so truthful, has been a part of the human experience for thousands of years. Recounting the particulars of an act or an event through the power of narrative continues to be one of the great aspects of relationships. It's another thing that sets us apart from animals. In journaling through Psalm 119, I came across a reference to story. As you read these selected verses, notice the word testimonies:

1 Blessed are those whose way is blameless,
Who walk in the Law of the LORD.
2 Blessed are those who comply with His testimonies,
And seek Him with all their heart
3 They also do no injustice;
They walk in His ways.
24 Your testimonies also are my delight;
They are my advisors.
46 I will also speak of Your testimonies before kings and shall not be ashamed.
59 I considered my ways
And turned my feet to Your testimonies
125 I am Your servant; give me understanding,
So that I may know Your testimonies.[1]

The Hebrew word for testimonies here is *edah*. It is chocked full of rich implications. First of all, it means testimony or witness – or story. *Edah* is always used to imply plural and divine – in other words, the testimonies, the stories of God. Also, it is meant to be repeated over and over. These are the stories of God that are to be shared again and again. Finally, these are stories that require an obedient response on the part of the listener. We are obligated to tell these stories, and the one who hears needs to decide how he or she will respond. That's a lot of meaning packed into one simple Hebrew word.

We always talk and make a big deal about our testimonies. But the bigger story here is obviously God's testimonies, His story, His *edah* – the story with the glorious ending, the story with so many twists and turns and unexpected shifts in the plot. So much laughter, so many tears, so much insight, so much ambiguity, so relational, so lonely, so much happiness, so much pain – and we get to be a part of it. All these many years of observing and participating in God's story make for one rich and meaningful journey through this life. I know that I'm much the better for it.

## And Now We Join This Program In Progress

The psalmist reminds us, *"Blessed [is the one] who observes His testimonies,"* who notices God's story, His *edah* happening all around. It would seem that the keys to happiness are none of the things advertised on television: good food and drink, a thicker, healthier head of hair, a slimmer, sleeker body, a cool car, or a house full of furniture that you don't have to start paying for until 2025. The key might very well be to give notice to God's story.

That brings me back to my original question: Am I self-centered or is it just me? We all are afflicted by huge doses of self-centeredness – like maybe the whole movie plot does revolve around us and our little part of the world. The truth is God's story is all around us and too often we're totally clueless and just too busy with our lives to notice. I read where the senior class motto for an upper scale high school in Dallas was "The lifestyles of the rich and clueless." Funny, creative, insightful, discouraging – all at the same time.

Andrew, one of our high school students, was sharing at our regular evening gathering. We were right there on the brink of the Rio Grande River, participating in our annual mission trip to a little border town. Everyone listened attentively as he talked about a conversation he had that day with a kid at Vacation Bible School. He said he was listening to a very needy person and searching for the right things to say in response, when, in his own words, "Something came over me. I guess it was...(a very long dramatic pause)...God!" Right there in front of us, he had one of those "Aha" moments. He was actually shocked as he made the connection. God's story was unfolding and he got to be a part of it. It was a God thing and he wasn't even aware of it until that very instance.

In *Five Smooth Stones for Pastoral Work*, Eugene Peterson goes to great depths to drive home the

importance of story. He stresses the utmost importance of helping others find their story – emphasizing
this as an intentional aspect of ministry with others.
It's not a sit still while I tell you a story to wow you
and inspire you, but rather a collaborative effort.
Peterson models it well, "We are going to talk
together, and we are going to make a story out of our
conversation. We are going to find out where we,
together, fit in the plot of God's story."[2] How exciting
is that – to lead kids to sense the ongoing story and
assist them in constructing the story they will tell as
part of the grand plot? Instead of just dropping your
three points to getting out of the mess they find
themselves in at the time, rather getting them to buy
into the grand narrative and the verse they'll
contribute.

It was after one of *The Lord of the Rings* movies.
There was a fairly good group of students and leaders
who came out for the midnight premiere. Afterwards, as we all gathered in the theater foyer,
someone asked me how I liked it. It came from
nowhere and made me instantly laugh at myself. "I
found parts of it hard to believe." It was funny
because it was so silly. It's *The Lord of the Rings* for
goodness sakes. It's fantasy. It's all made up – with
hobbits and wizards and elves. But what was funnier
to me were those in our group who went, "Yeah, I
know what you mean." It's always fun to play around
with some of the unbelievable purveyors of gullibility

that we get to work with. But the point here is basically if you don't get emotionally involved in a story
like *The Lord of the Rings*, it's going to seem so foolish.
You have to totally buy into the story.

It's okay to see God's *edah* in the trees and hills
and sunsets and the stars, even in the mysterious
adventure of Providence. Just make sure as you turn
your mind's attention toward His story, that you also
turn your heart's affection toward His narrative as
well. Listening wholeheartedly – with mind and heart.
John Piper says that truth [mind] without emotion
[heart] produces artificial admirers – like those who
write the messages on greeting cards.[3] I saw a
greeting card with this message inscribed, "My love,
my life, my happiness. You are all things beautiful to
me." That's a beautiful collection of words, but they
were written by some paid employee just trying to
make a buck and, therefore, are not from the heart.
The one who is blessed is the one whose quest it is to
seek God with all his or her mind and heart. One
without the other seldom finds anything worth
having. In fact, it shows contempt for God. The
sacred quest would be to listen intently and wholeheartedly to His *edah*. Listen with your brain, use
your reason and intellect, but also listen with your
heart. And help kids do the same – observe and
listen.

How cool it is for those in youth ministry to be
surrounded by a panoramic view of God's story in

progress. There's nothing better than when students you encounter along the youth ministry journey blow you away with a contribution to the ongoing story. One day, fifteen-year-old Cydney walked up and handed me an envelope. Inside was a nice card with some kind words and a thousand-dollar check (from her own account). It was a donation to our youth fund to buy much needed sound equipment. She had received some money from her grandmother and wanted to give some of it right back to the church. What a lesson from a kid who didn't have much but just wanted to be faithful.

I took the check and thanked her repeatedly, and I even shared her story a number of times. I also hope I was listening carefully as she was trying to write a new chapter in her spiritual pilgrimage. That's something we aren't always good at – listening. Every good story (or just a work in progress) needs a good listener. Peterson mandates that we have to listen and help these we serve work out their stories, show them how to rearrange some of the details and even point out some things they might have missed. We have to believe that there is a story to be told, and we have to convince this generation of the same thing. It's so crucial for students as we live in these times.

I stood on the South Padre Island beach with a bunch of my seniors. It was a late Sunday evening, and we sang worship songs as the ocean breeze opened up waves of adoration for our Creator. As I strummed my guitar, I looked at the faces of students who were just days before receiving their diplomas. I saw students who had been able to flourish spiritually throughout those prime suffering years of junior high and high school – not just survive, but live well, pretty much avoiding the trappings of what is paraded as the necessities of high school pleasures. I looked upon students who had finished strong, whose legacy, whose story was set to serve as a model of how kids can basically cruise through these adolescent years and skip all the arduous detours of excess and abuse and lost innocence. Another chapter was added to God's story. But then I watched as some from this "trophy class" took off for college and struggled. Watching graduates of your ministry lose their faith, choose very different paths, or any combination thereof is disconcerting to say the least. It makes me wonder if I didn't listen enough.

With a front row seat afforded to us as youth workers, it's our privilege and responsibility to notice the ongoing story, recognize its origin, get involved, and help kids find their story, even as ours is expanding. American folk singer Pete Seeger took an interesting slant when he said, "I don't know what the fate of the human race is, but I do know that if we make it, it will be because we tell our stories." We do have some knowledge of that fate, but it doesn't negate the absolute need to tell our stories.

· · ·

## "I Hate My Life"

"Every happening, great and small, is a parable whereby God speaks to us, and the art of life is to get the message."[4] Malcolm Muggeridge said it, and I believe it. Melody's status update on Facebook was probably an impulsive, reactionary blurt – yet there it was for all to see, "I hate my life." You don't have to do much reading between the lines on that one. Melody continued, "I wish I had different parents and I really mean it!" I was quickly getting a good sense of the plot line of Melody's story.

All stories have conflict, potential for disaster and a possible sad ending (even Disney movies). I remember sitting with my wife Debbie in the theater years ago and watching a Disney classic, *White Fang*. In the climactic scene, it appears that White Fang (a wolf, befriended and domesticated by a boy) is dead. I was a little misty-eyed and Debbie was quietly crying and reaching for a tissue. But the kid behind me was weeping and looking for consolation from his mom. "Please Mom," he begged out loud, "tell me White Fang is going to be okay!" I have to admit that the kid was getting to me. I wanted to assure him that all Disney movies have happy endings. But then I wasn't really sure. Remember Bambi's mother? That one has scarred kids for years. But then at the perfect moment, White Fang bursts into the clearing and leaps into the arms of his boy master. A perfect, happy ending – just like we all wanted. I always wondered what would have happened to the crying kid if Disney had chosen to have White Fang locked on the boy's throat instead. But that's weird.

The happy ending is something we all desire. They all lived happily ever after. In a movie or a book, the suspension of disbelief can wreak havoc on our emotions. It's also what makes the story so much better. As you find yourself immersed emotionally at a deep level, you keep wondering where will this story take us? As you sit with a student and listen as they unlock secrets (often for the first time), you know this story can have a good ending. You just want the kid to believe that too. Helping kids see the mess they find themselves in as a part of the bigger story is the plan. It starts by being a determined listener. When instructing his students in medical school, French physician Laennec used to maintain, "Listen, listen to your patient! He is giving you the diagnosis."

I got a call from Charmaine. She was in the bathroom, with the door locked, and she had just taken a handful of pills. "What should I do?" she implored. I pleaded with her to go tell her parents. She refused. No way to call since she was using the home phone. So here I found myself driving to Charmaine's house, thinking about what had brought her to this point. Her story took a detour into the unhealthy relationship department. By giving herself away sexually, she had plenty of boyfriends and a stout reputation to go with it. It had worked for awhile. But it wasn't working any more. As I stood with her parents in the ER and watched her being forced to throw-up all those pills, it was obvious that she was losing her story. It was slipping through her fingers. Maybe Melody, who was Facebooking the disdain she had for her life, was on the verge of doing the same thing.

## Denarrated...

Shakespeare states emphatically that all the world's a stage – that we are all merely players, with different entrances and exits. As life's story unfolds, we play different parts. William refers to the various stages as "The Seven Ages of Man." These are the periods in a man's life: his years as an infant, a schoolboy, a lover, a soldier, a judge, a foolish old man, and finally "second childishness and mere oblivion"[5] – without teeth, without eyes, without taste, without everything. May I add something else we are in danger of being without? We could end up without a story!

In Doug Coupland's quirky *Polaroids from the Dead*, he makes up a new word. You won't find it in the dictionary, but it should be. The word is "denarration." He talks about the deep need that we all have for our lives to be stories or narratives. But there is the possibility that our stories may vanish, just disappear. And when that happens, "we feel lost, dangerous, out of control, and susceptible to the forces of randomness."[6] When a person loses his or her life story, we have another victim of denarration. Another way of saying, "not having a life." Coupland continues, "It became possible to be alive yet have no religion, no family connections, no ideology, no sense of class location, no politics, and no sense of history. No story."[7] Denarrated!

What a mandate youth workers have to help kids avoid being denarrated. Of course, we have to first make sure we don't lose our story in the process. One of the Polaroid snapshots provided in the book was one from the beautiful life of singer/actor Dean Martin:

> "Beautiful. It's great. I wake up every morning.
> Massive bowel movement. The Mexican maid
> makes me some breakfast. Down to the club here.
> At least nine holes. A nice lunch. Go home, sit by
> the TV. The Mexican maid makes me a nice
> dinner. A few drinks. Go to bed. Wake
> up the next morning. Another massive bowel
> movement. Beautiful. This is my life."[8]

Just a few short years later, Martin was a "walking corpse," as he continued drinking himself to an early grave. His beautiful narrative had imploded. Denarrated!

We all have the potential to be denarrated, especially when we attempt to extract ourselves from

God's story – leaving us sliding down a slippery slope towards a life that is plotless. There is the story of God's faithfulness – still we find ourselves taking matters into our own hands, and kind of forgetting to seek His direction and blessing. There is the story of God's love – still we find ourselves withholding love from kids who bug us, even as we intensely love others. There is the story of God's hope – still we find ourselves fretting over an uncertain future, especially as we get older. There is the story of God's peace and comfort – still we find ourselves trying to make life more comfortable through activity and things. Look out! Those are some of the ingredients for a lost story.

In a personal favorite, *A Severe Mercy*, Sheldon Vanauken teetered on the edge of being denarrated. "I didn't want God aboard. He was too heavy. I wanted Him approving from a distance…like a loved poem I could read when I wanted to. I didn't want to be swallowed up in God. I wanted holidays from the school of Christ."[9] This continues to be a huge temptation for the kids we work with. Too many want just enough of Christ to stay comfortable. But to take a holiday, a sabbatical from God's story, to take off on our own, leaves you like a kite that pulls itself away from the string. It just never works out like you planned.

. . .

## Not With A Whimper But A Bang

In making my way through Chesterton's incredibly thick, *Everlasting Man*, I came across this quote that adds much to this discussion. "Yet the whole trouble comes from a man trying to look at these stories from the outside, as if they were scientific objects. He has only to look at them from the inside and ask himself how he would begin the story. A story may start with anything and go anywhere."[10] I was standing in a Namibian airport with twenty of my high school students, getting ready to make our way home from a mission trip. Colleen, standing in line next to me, noticed the combination lock imbedded in a friend's Samsonite suitcase. Out of curiosity, she casually asked, "Does that show how many miles the bag has gone?" It did look very much like an odometer. At first, I thought she was joking and laughed, but then quickly realized she wasn't joking and laughed even harder.

I love that story and have told it many times. But that's really just the beginning of the story. As Chesterton so astutely noted how a story may start with anything and go in many directions, I have witnessed that in Colleen's life. Starting with a mission trip to Africa, the story continues, to this day, of a girl who had a massive paradigm shift in the way she viewed this world we live in – and how actively God was involved in it all. Here was a spiritual lightweight flying across the ocean on an adventure but coming back with a new heart fixed on the Father – and a new, deep passion to be involved in His story (like teaching Muslim children in the middle east for three years after college).

I love T.S. Eliot's insightful poem, *The Hollow Men*. Here are some excerpts:

We are the hollow men
We are the stuffed men
Leaning together
Headpiece filled with straw. Alas!
Our dried voices, when
We whisper together
Are quiet and meaningless
As wind in dry grass
Or rats' feet over broken glass
In our dry cellar
Shape without form, shade without colour,
Paralyzed force, gesture without motion;
Those who have crossed
With direct eyes, to death's other Kingdom
Remember us – if at all – not as lost
Violent souls, but only
As the hollow men
The stuffed men[11]

And then the poem ends with these words: "This is the way the world ends – Not with a bang but a whimper." To think one's story would end up like the hollow men – not with a bang, but with a whimper – without shape, without colour, locked up and going nowhere – now that would be a sad state of affairs.

The Psalmist says, *"For all our days have dwindled away in Your fury; We have finished our years like a sigh."* Alas, we have finished our years like a sigh. Kind of like a whimper. He continues, *"Teach us to number our days, that we may present to You a heart of wisdom."*[12] To number our days, not to finish our years like a sigh – that sounds too much like settling. A sigh is content-ment that has been too heavily saturated with complacency – like a cancer eating away at inner passions for life and adventure. A sigh is a resignation to sitting on a folding chair at the very edge of the dance floor, longingly watching the dancers, but never joining in – although there is a toe tapping that wants its attached body to shed its onerous hesitation and join in. To number our days is to be imbued with life's rhythm with a carefree nature like a merry fiddler who plays his notes as fast as he can, not because he has to, but because he wants to – and because he can. Every invitation to join in with the chorus that we spurn is another day that has flown away, never to be recaptured. It's a sigh of resignation that comes from a hollow person with no shape, no purpose. What's the point?

Chesterton again, "You cannot finish a sum how you like. But you can finish a story how you like."[13] He goes on to note the difference between calculus and Shakespeare's Romeo and Juliet. One can't change the rules of math, but Shakespeare could have had Romeo marry his old nurse if he had decided so. The call of God is for all Christians, not just a few bold, radical, really out-going believers, but all. How will your story end? What verse will you contribute? Will they say, "This is how your life ended, not with a whimper, but a bang"?

One of our students had a near-tragic accident a few years ago. Scott sustained a spinal cord injury that left him with some partial (and eventually temporary) paralysis. One of our volunteers, Jonathan, and I stood by his bed in the ICU room one evening. Jonathan had brought a CD player to the bay and was playing the soundtrack to *Braveheart.* It was good pump up music for Scott who was already dead-set on being an overcomer. As we were quietly talking, Scott noted that the "Freedom" song was playing. He decided that he and Jonathan were going to shout "Freedom!" at the exact moment in the music when Mel Gibson's character does so in the movie. I informed them both that it's usually not a good idea to shout things in an ICU ward. So they agreed that they would just speak the exclamation in a more hushed, yet still emphatic manner. It was already a glimpse into the resiliency that Scott would have in the months to come.

About this time, one of the hospital chaplains came into the bay. He was younger, probably still in training. He began his chaplain banter with Scott, who was barely aware of his presence. Instead, Scott was holding Jonathan's hand and waiting for the squeeze that would signify the cue for the quiet shout. I thought to myself, "This is going to be good." The poor chaplain was waxing eloquently when the music finally reached the appropriate crescendo and a much louder than expected "Freedom!" came forth from their lips. They obviously didn't cover this in his CPE classes, because the visibly shaken chaplain stammered out a few concluding words and made a quick exit possibly to go look for a patient who was heavily sedated instead.

I see this as another beautiful, perfectly written chapter in God's story. Scott went on to be an inspiration with his strong faith and God-empowered determination to get back up on his feet. After high school, he became a great volunteer and helped disciple high school boys for several years. But I will always remember his shout of freedom. There was no whimper there, not at all. Only a bang! This is such clear evidence of the Storyteller who is crafting a masterpiece and allowing us to be a part of it. How great is that? It's what we carry from each day lived. The stories of adventure and love, of beauty and pain, of inspiration and disappointment. God's stories told and retold by those who saw and heard are what sustain us and encourage us and humor us and teach us. It's why we live.

# Chapter Nine

# THE SKY IS FALLING, THE SKY IS FALLING

*The point of having an open mind, like having an open
mouth, is to close it on something solid.*
G. K. Chesterton

Okay, I admit it. I really don't like jazz. I've actually
tried. It's not hip not to like jazz. Guess what? After
reading Donald Miller's super hipster *Blue Like Jazz*
years ago, I gave it another shot. Downloaded a Miles
Davis album and gave it a listen. Just couldn't get into
it. It's not the musicianship. Are there any better
musicians than jazz players? No! And Miller makes it
sound so cool. It's America's music, "birthed out of
freedom."[1] Lots of notes and fusion (whatever that
means) and soul. Still I prefer the simplicity and
rawness of rock 'n' roll, even though, pound for

pound, jazz musicians leave their rocker counterparts in the dust. But I've been that way ever since I heard my first Beatles' song. I don't want to get into a debate about jazz vs. rock. I just wanted to say that I really don't like jazz.

I remember quite well reading books by Donald Miller, Anne Lamott, Brian McLaren, Rob Bell, and other quasi-iconoclastic authors who always made me think as they rattled the cage of 21$^{st}$ century Christianity. The mixture of pure talent, refreshing vulnerability, and ingenious perspective found me jotting down excerpts into my journal for future reference. Obviously, this is true for lots of people. These modern-day crusaders were passionately tearing down institutional Christianity limb by limb, prophesying the impending demise of said institution. Hey, they made great sense...some of the time.

Now the following is just my opinion. And opinions are just like butts. Everyone has one, and you can always find cracks in them. So like the plumber squatting down in the kitchen, you can focus on the perceived cracks in my logic, or you can just give an objective listen to these ramblings. Here goes...

Is the church as we know it on life support? Is the sky really falling? Will a new postmodern paradigm of ministry totally eradicate the present ecclesiastical structure and finally fulfill the Great Commission the way Christ intended? Who knows? We're all taking a huge educated guess at it, aren't we?

. . .

## What Will People Think When They Hear That I'm A Jesus Freak?

My only frame of reference with the prognostications of these present-day reformers will have to be what I experienced in the very early '70s. There was a noteworthy awakening that was taking place in America at the time. It was called the Jesus Movement. Youth Ministry veteran, Dawson McAllister, put it succinctly that the church was so dead that God did an end run around the church by using kids outside its walls. A spiritual renaissance erupted within the so-called hippie movement — and it was real. I remember going to a Christian Woodstock-like deal in Dallas called Explo '72. It was the most people I've ever seen in one place. If my memory serves me correct, there were close to 200,000 people at the all-day music festival. This was some serious trailblazing on the part of Campus Crusade, as they culturally embraced rock 'n' roll and the counter culture that was continually evolving around it. Bill Bright and Billy Graham were there to completely validate this new expression. To say the least, Christians everywhere had to sit up and take notice.

When I originally wrote this chapter, I found it quite surreal that Larry Norman, one of my musical heroes, featured on the program at Explo '72, and right in the huge middle of this Jesus Movement, actually passed away at the age of 60. I was saddened to hear that his voice was finally silenced, although not completely. I have six of his albums in my iTunes library. At the time, I actually did something quite pointless. I posted a tribute to him on the wall of my Facebook page for students everywhere to quickly ignore and move on to more pressing matters, like joining the "I Just Had a Socially Awkward Moment with a Squirrel" group (which at that time had 698 members). Larry's relevance was shocking to mainstream Christianity as he attempted to bring Jesus to kids in the streets. He was arguably the original "Jesus Freak", a term coined during that same era. Constantly criticized by Christians everywhere, he never gave up in his attempt to use music the way I believe Jesus would have used it. I choose to believe that if Jesus had been a musician in this era, He would have probably never recorded a "worship" album. I believe He would have made music like this.

'Cause I've been in your churches and sat in your pews
And heard sermons on just how much money you'll need for the year.
And I've heard you make reference to Mexicans, Chinamen, N----rs, and Jews
And I gather you wish we would all disappear
And you call yourselves Christians, when really you're not,
You're living your life as you please.

If you're really a Christian, then put down
yourself
And follow wherever God leads.
*Right Here In America*, Larry Norman 1970[2]

These words were representative of many of the attitudes prevalent among the young Christians who unofficially aligned themselves with the Jesus Movement.

In 1969, the music minister at my Southern Baptist church asked me to bring my acoustic guitar to the Sunday evening service. He wanted to try out a Christian folk song with our youth choir. I thought he was crazy. Was he looking for trouble and possible unemployment? I had visions of the pastor ceremoniously telling this maverick not to let the door hit him where the good Lord split him. But my friend Phil and I did play our six strings on that landmark night, accompanying the memorable *Andrew Told His Brother, Have You Told Yours?* and no one swooned or stood up and tore his leisure suit from his chest at such a blasphemous act. People weren't happy about it. But pretty soon we were bringing electric guitars and drum kits and playing extremely soft, soft rock songs with sanctified lyrics on Sunday evenings. Sounds almost silly now, but it was quite revolutionary back then.

Point? Well, all this stuff was happening. Radical

stuff to say the least. We all thought that church as we knew it was going to change dramatically – all for the good. The church did change, but the church also continued on. Like a gigantic ocean liner, the bow kept furrowing through the waters of twentieth century faith. The rudder was adjusted a bit as things began to go in a slightly different direction. The ripples of that change can be felt today. But one thing is for sure. The mighty ship didn't sink to the bottom of sea of irrelevancy. There was not another sleek, new vessel built in its place.

## The Truth Is Out There

Now no one is probably any more enamored with cultural relevancy than me. I pursue that and have gotten in trouble more than once for that passionate pursuit – like the Wednesday night when the "S" word reverberated loudly through our PA system. My associate, future SkitGuy, Eddie James, rewound the movie clip just a little bit too far. But I keep hearing the tones of a kind of relevancy that bother me. In the drive to be culturally relevant, there is often an obsession to find truth in the strangest of places. These are voices that are decrying the fascist, morality driven forces of ministry that are being exposed for all their manipulative, almost injurious techniques. No argument here about the fact that there continues to be guilt merchants throughout

Christendom, peddling their brand of culpability to the masses. You know who they are. I remember sitting in a huge rally and listening to a preacher tell stories of bus wrecks and incinerated kids. As he weaved a tale of manipulation and as hundreds of students who did not want anything to do with being reduced to ashes in a bus or elsewhere flowed down the aisle, I felt as if I should rush the stage, give a round house kick to this charlatan, and grab the microphone and mention a few words about grace.

But I think the accusation against moral policemen in the church is also directed at those of us who, along with a steady diet of grace talk, felt the distinct need to help kids discover moral parameters during the time we had with them. The indictment stated that if I did that, then I was doing irreparable damage to them. What? We can't ever say "No" to kids? We're not supposed to suggest, "Hey, make good choices out there"? Are you kidding? We're supposed to let them discover Jesus, but not encounter some of the tough words that came from His lips? He did talk about denial, and about lust, and about going and sinning no more, didn't He?

It's been said that ministers should be careful not to set up parameters, build walls that inhibit the opportunity for students to experience Jesus. Chesterton in Orthodoxy beautifully rebuts this idea:

"...doctrine and discipline may be walls; but they are the walls of a playground....We might fancy some children playing on the flat grassy top of some tall island in the sea. So long as there was a wall around the cliff's edge they could fling themselves into every frantic game and make the place the noisiest of nurseries. But the walls were knocked down, leaving the naked peril of the precipice. They did not fall over; but when their friends returned to them they were all huddled in terror in the center of the island; and their song had ceased."[3]

Thank you Gilbert! This is the well-painted picture of the playground of faith, of the song and dance of mysterious and unpredictable spirituality, but with some built-in protection. Why not? Why should we be wary of talking of discipline within the Christian life? Why should we shy away from teaching of the safeguards that God felt was so important that He engraved them into stone...twice?

Check out what C.S. Lewis said about the subject. "Some modern theologians have, quite rightly, protested against an excessively moralistic interpretation of Christianity...God may be more than moral goodness: He is not less. The road to the promised land runs past Sinai."[4] Well played – and just as relevant today as it was fifty years ago when it was written. There is room for both – in fact, there is an absolute need for both. I cannot, I will not apologize for upholding the banner of morality for students to behold and to strive for in their spiritual journey. We should stay committed to teaching the "Thou shalts" continually and with great forthrightness in our presentations, but we must not neglect the "Thou shalt nots" as well. We do our students a great disservice if we choose otherwise.

This debate goes hand in hand with today's great drive toward the ultimate in cultural relevancy in ministry. It really does. The withholding of nothing from your eyes in the quest to find truth is quite popular in this day and time. I listened to one of my friends complain about the morality-driven youth ministry he grew up in, even as he talked about all the movies he saw and the benefits of truth discovered within even the most R-rated of them. He reiterated the fact that churches must stop drawing lines, setting moral parameters for people – but almost within the same breath mentioned that, of course, one shouldn't go to pornography for the purpose of truth-finding. I thought to myself, "Didn't he just draw a line?" Then I answered myself, "Yes, he did!" It hit me. We all set parameters. We do. The argument isn't over the setting of moral boundaries, but over the location.

It's not really that we tear down the walls around the playground that our students recreate within, but where we position those walls. Some may say they want to tear them all down. Actually they are just pushing them out to the point that they are barely perceptible. But the walls are there still the same.

## So Open-Minded That His Brains Leaked Out

The Old Testament Hebrews mingled with the nations, and learned their practices, and served their idols. They invaded and dwelt within a new land and a new culture. Their goal should have been to be in the culture but not to serve the culture and bow down to its gods. It would appear that too many Christians are falling into that trap! Whenever you leave the safety of the fold and strive to connect with those outside the bubble, there is always the possibility of casualties – or at least watered-down Christianity that no longer has any taste – like Coke with all the ice melted and the fizz gone. Tasteless Christianity needs something, stronger doses of culture. But it still needs an edge to it, especially if you think of it as forcing the round peg of Christianity into the square hole of culture. We have to be out there, hammering that peg into the world. There is a chance that that hole is going to splinter a bit with some of the tough dialogue. But to plane down Christian conviction so that it fits rather nicely seems to contradict the claims of Christ. One author talked of a pastor who "became so much like the culture in which he lived that in his relevance he became irrelevant."[5]

When my daughter was six years old, I watched with great interest as she entered a kiddie maze in the Looney Tunes section of Six Flags. The walls of the maze were tall enough to shield her vision, but short enough for me to see her. When she got confused, I started to carefully guide her through the rest of the maze. "Hannah, go to your right! Now turn the corner! No, go the other direction!" She knew her father's voice, trusted my directions, and came out at the end, leaping into my arms – quite proud of her accomplishment. Now if she had ignored my instructions and corrections, there was a chance that she would have exited much later – and not nearly as happy. I know this analogy falls to pieces with too much scrutiny. But let's not go there. Just suffice it to say that heeding the Father's admonitions are key ingredients to living large.

The book of John informs us that many believed Jesus but would not confess it for fear that they might be kicked out of the synagogue. The problem was they *"loved the approval of men rather than the approval of God."*[6] This fear of spiritual transparency continues on until the present day. Isn't it the approval of men that often fills the sails of cultural relevancy? The motive may have been well founded, but too often at the core is fear, the fear of being exposed as an evangelical Christian and being put out of the synagogue of politically correct spiritual-speak (or just popular public opinion). Wasn't Jesus Christ the most relevant man ever to live? Fear of being put out of the synagogue (something He literally faced throughout) never reared its ugly head as He continued living out the Father's will. Being caught up in the pursuit of man's approval can catch us choosing words "too wisely," tap dancing around spiritual truths that need to be addressed. It's an easy trap to fall into. I do it regularly. Heart-felt motives. Good intentions galore. Too often a divine encounter missed. Pretty soon, we find ourselves referring to the New Testament as two thousand year old letters that are just a bit out of touch.[7] And just like that, we lose our place at the table and our opportunity to join in the conversation. In the search for relevance, we become irrelevant.

John Stott firmly states, "The great tragedy in the church today is that evangelicals are biblical, but not contemporary, while liberals are contemporary, but not biblical. We need faithfulness to the ancient word and sensitivity to the modern world." I love how many ministers describe themselves as theologically conservative and culturally liberal. In my humble opinion, it's the best of both worlds. And a winning combination. In working with students, it's the perfect formula to enable them to encounter Christ and His claims.

Back to Chesterton again: "A man must be interested in life...the heart must be fixed on the right thing. The moment we have a fixed heart, we have a free hand."[8] He goes on to tell the story of a middle-aged man who had two wives, one that was older than him and the other younger. As his hair began turning grey, the younger wife didn't like it. So every night she pulled out the grey ones. On the other hand, the older wife enjoyed the fact that he was turning grey, since she didn't like being mistaken for his mother. So every morning as she combed his hair, she plucked out some of the black ones. I guess you can guess the end result. The man soon found himself completely bald. "Yield to all and you will soon have nothing to yield."[9] It was Steve Taylor who coined the lyric, "You're so open-minded that your brains leaked out."[10] There is absolutely nothing wrong with trying to intellectualize our faith and even attempting to articulate our spiritual hipness. I'm okay with that. Just don't miss the point of it all. If, at the end of the day, all you have is a generous mishmash of contradictory spiritual values – a kind of a what will be will be theology, then what's the point?

### We Don't Need No Institutions

Of course, the anti-institutional dialogue is very much intertwined with this topic of discussion. It's about deconstructing the church as an institution. A kind of spiritual anarchy if you choose. It's the cry of outrage against the institutional church. Been there, done that. I certainly find myself on the deconstruction crew on a regular basis in conversations with others, especially as I find many of our students not engaged in our church's worship services on a weekly basis. Let's level this puppy, eliminate anything that smacks of institution, and do "church" right for a change. Why not? Sometimes a house is just too far gone to be repaired and remodeled. Take it down to the foundation and rebuild.

I was sharing lunch with Jim, one of our former students and, at the time, working as a small group leader in our ministry. He was talking about the house church he and some other Baylor students had started. They were meeting in someone's apartment once a week to share a meal and spiritual ideas. He was decreeing that this was their "church" – as he threw out dogmatic assertions that this body would never become institutionalized. I loved his enthusiasm because I like stuff like this. I really do. My friend Greg, the Eddie Van Halen disciple referred to earlier, pastored a church like this in Austin, and he was reaching people most churches could never reach. But I asked Jim some simple questions: Do you hope your church will reach new people and grow? Of course! What happens if you grow to the point that you have to start meeting in the clubhouse at the apartment complex? And then all of a sudden, someone has to get there early to set up chairs...and couples get married and start dropping babies and a nursery is needed...aren't you becoming institutionalized to some degree? Our conversation quickly moved in a new direction.

All I am saying is that I don't really like jazz, but I have a deep, profound respect for it. So why can't we all just get along? Stop setting up lines of demarcation, declaring any way to do church as antiquated and on life support or just too cutting edge or anywhere in between.

I find it interesting that our youth ministry continues to explore ancient forms of worship, and we're not the only ones for sure. By the way, the response has been outstanding. We have what we call Midnight Mass every night at camp (it actually starts at 11:00). We clear the room, set up tons of candles, play Gregorian chants, flash meditative scriptures at the front, and watch in amazement as scores of teenagers quietly enter with journals and Bibles and pillows—and just bask in the solitude of the moment.

I like the concept that Stephen Covey introduced in *Seven Habits of Highly Effective People*. He calls it valuing your differences. The application is simple. It means not using different opinions of church and spirituality as points of conflict, but rather finding value in what a baby boomer brings to the table and also finding value in the fresh perspective of a Gen X'er and the overwhelmingly hipster ideas of the Millennial and so on. I read, with great interest, about a ministry symposium where some of the participants publicly complained about the boomers who were present. The question was what did they know about reaching these younger generations? Oh, such arrogance! But I also heard of a pastor of a large church who threatened his staff with expulsion if they were caught reading any of Brian McLaren's books. A mandate based in fear, no doubt. A bit of silliness if I should say so myself. We should always read books we don't necessarily agree with. That's a no-brainer. Let's face the truth: a little mutual respect between young church leaders and old church leaders would do us all good as we find value in each other.

Hey, the sky may be falling. A look across the landscape of Christianity in America can be discouraging. The statistics can be downright depressing. Can they ever! I do know that the answers are going to be difficult. But in the words of the classic *High School Musical*, "We're all in this together." Sorry for the cheesy cliché ending to this important chapter, but that really is true. We're all in this together, and at the end of the day, we've still got God! I like our odds.

# Chapter Ten

# AND SO ON AND SO FORTH...

*"I rant, therefore I am."*
Dennis Miller

Here is a chapter dedicated to the rants and ramblings of an old youth pastor. It's a collection of little snippets on various and sundry subjects – observations made on this brilliant journey I've been on for the overwhelming majority of my adult life. So let the rambling begin...

## Disposable Worship

Let me help you see where I'm coming from. During his Baylor University days, David Crowder played keyboards in my Wednesday night band.

That's right, he wasn't a guitarist back then, but rather, a pretty darn good piano player. Weekly he stood behind his keys, with a ball cap pulled down over his eyes, and quietly played his part. We didn't even give him a microphone. I didn't know he could sing. He actually learned how to play guitar on my well-traveled Takamine, which I had to go retrieve a year later at his apartment. During that time, I couldn't believe how good he got – blew right past me on the six-string highway. After the formation of the David Crowder Band, he still came over for two and a half years and led worship for our small group ministry. Jack Parker played lead guitar in our band for several years. That's where he and Crowder met and later formed the David Crowder Band. Now he tours with Chris Tomlin. Eric Clapton and Jack are two of my guitar heroes.

Speaking of Chris Tomlin, he led worship for our summer camp for eight years. I like to remind him that the very first time we had him at our camp he was our fifth choice. The first four guys were already booked. I had never actually met him face to face before that first year. When Chris walked up to introduce himself that first day of camp, I thought he was a student from another church. I remember thinking, what have we gotten ourselves into? Louie Giglio was our speaker that year and had voiced some concern over this new guy as the worship leader. I was trying to spin it with Louie, but inside I had the same concerns. That worked out pretty well for both of us. Did I mention that Louie used to be a member of my church here in Waco?

Presently, Logan Walter is a gifted worship leader in the Dallas area. When Logan was a freshman in high school, I installed him as (in his words) "the back-up acoustic guitarist"—and used to show him stuff on the guitar. Yeah, right! Another one left me eating his dust. Same thing with Art Wellborn who is presently leading our youth worship and is freakishly talented.

Okay, what's the point of all this? It's really not to show off. I promise. My first rant is about what I call disposable worship. I've talked with all the aforementioned fellows about what I perceive as a long-term problem. In dialogue with these guys, I have wondered out loud if a legacy of worship is in serious jeopardy for this generation.

Here's the progression of worship in my lifetime: Hymns and more hymns, played as fast as possible with a couple of moms on piano and organ...almost always, the first, second, and last verses. Then came the choruses with guitars and, later on, the drums. The first choruses to hit it big were all really short: *I Love You Lord, More Precious Than Silver, My Only Hope Is You, O Lord You're Beautiful*. These were some of the most popular.

I do remember when the pastor at my church in the early '80s decided to introduce some of these new choruses to the church. Since I was the only one who knew how to play them (there was little sheet music back then, just chords scratched down on a piece of paper), he asked me to help. It was the first big night of our revival, and we would lead the choruses while the choir was getting warmed up for the service. We chose three, but because they were so short, we finished before the choir was ready. In the awkward silence, he stepped over to the piano and whispered for me to play a hymn until the choir came in. Well, my background was rock and roll, so I whispered back, "I don't know any hymns." His solution, "Well, play something." So as the sounds of silence penetrated the packed worship center, I reluctantly launched into an obscure Beatles' song off the *White Album*. Only the most hard-core Beatles fan would have recognized it. I played the entire song, and still no choir. Now I was stuck and found myself playing *Wild World* by Cat Stevens. Even though I tried to tone it down, I could see people recognizing the ill-fitted song and laughing, as they enjoyed my predicament. Finally, the choir came out, which was good. My next choice was going to be a churchified version of *Stairway To Heaven*.

Like I said, the choruses were short. But then great songwriters started writing full-blown songs of worship which required overhead projectors and transparencies. That was cool, but PowerPoint was going to be a lot cooler. *All In All, His Banner Over*

*Me, I Just Wanna Be Where You Are*, and other great songs came along. Praise teams started springing up in the most traditional of churches, blended worship became a new catch phrase, and the raging debate between traditional and contemporary continued on. *God Of Wonders, My Glorious, You Alone, We Fall Down* were just some of our kids' favorites.

We continued on into postmodern worship – with the new mixed in with a profound interest in the old and ancient. It was exciting and invigorating. Crowder, Tomlin, and others revived old hymns and endeared them to new generations, while introducing us to new songs. Matt Redman's *Ten Thousand Reasons* and John Mark McMillan's *How He Loves* were personal favorites and were, for a while, in heavy rotation with our praise band. To this day, the timeline of worship music goes on and on.

And your point is? Well my point is as we are using up worship songs and disposing of them at such a rapid pace, is the lack of a worship legacy unimportant? Look at the songs I listed in the last couple of paragraphs. They are almost all basically non-existent presently. Already it feels like *Ten Thousand Reasons* and *How He Loves* have fallen into the same category. Is that okay? These were songs, written by godly men and women who were obviously inspired by the Holy Spirit to put down words to great tunes, to be used to help Christians in Louie Giglio's words to, "turn your mind's attention and your heart's affection toward God."

Is this a problem? I think so. Three or four times a year, I get my rock and roll fix by playing with the band at our Wednesday night outreach. I remember when we did *Hey Jude* as an opener. It was great. The crowd swarmed up around the stage and sang, uproariously the repetitious, yet catchy "Na, na, na..." ending to the song. It was recorded in 1968. At that time, all of my students were born in the late 1990s and early 2000s. What's the deal? The deal is the song has stood the test of time. Have none of these great worship songs stood the test of time? Apparently not, but I think it's not necessarily the fault of the song. It's our collective fault.

I think that youth workers and worship leaders should be intentional in refusing just to use up the newest and the best and then throwing it away when the next newest and best comes along. When Crowder led worship for us at the turn of the millennium, we regularly sang his *All I Can Say*. It quickly became one of our favorites. Just a few weeks ago, and years later, we sang *All I Can Say* during our small group worship time. We are probably the only youth ministry in the world that sings that song, but it remains part of our legacy of worship. That's what I'm talking about. Once I asked Art, our most excellent worship associate, to put *Did You Feel The Mountains Tremble?* by Delirious into the set. The kids loved it, wanted to know the name so they could download it. Some songs need to be disposed of, and I won't be crass and name names right here. You are probably thinking of some good examples even now. But there are some songs that should not be forgotten. That is our responsibility to determine the songs that have stood the test of time. Think about senior adults who could sing forever, from memory, all the hymns of old. When these generations are older, will they ever be able to sing anything without words on a screen? It's something to think about.

When U2's 360° tour came through Dallas, I was there. Amazing! After the band played their most excellent song *One*, Bono started singing *Amazing Grace*. Eighty-thousand people joined right in. It was beautiful. First and last verses. A song for the ages. A song that has stood the test of time. As we lead our ministries, we must be good stewards in helping our kids come away with songs to be sung for a lifetime.

## Pastoral Authority

I grow weary of hearing ministers trashing their pastors. It's pretty epidemic. I always find it particularly interesting when one fellow keeps crapping out on the pastor lottery. Every church this one goes to has a pastor who is micro-managing, a terrible preacher, demanding, and/or insecure about having such a dynamic, well-loved youth pastor on his staff.

I'm not saying those kind of pastors aren't out there. You and I both know they are. It's just when it keeps happening to the same person, maybe one should look in the mirror to see part of the problem.

One issue I see is how quickly folks will speak poorly about their pastors, eviscerating them at the drop of a hat. I'm always reminded of what happened with David and Saul in 1 Samuel 26:

> So David and Abishai came to the people by night, and behold, Saul lay sleeping inside the circle of the camp with his spear stuck in the ground at his head; and Abner and the people were lying around him. Then Abishai said to David, "Today God has handed your enemy over to you; now then, please let me pin him with the spear to the ground with one thrust, and I will not do it to him a second time." But David said to Abishai, "Do not kill him, for who can reach out his hand against the LORD'S anointed and remain innocent?"[1]

Not being a hermeneutical first stringer doesn't disqualify me from taking a stab at seeing a very transferable concept in this passage. Saul was the anointed king, but he was far, far outside of God's will at this stage of the game. David was fleeing for his life, literally. Saul wasn't trying to micro-manage David. He was trying to macro-murder him. Here was David's chance to take him out. But he asked a very thought-provoking question, "Who can stretch out his hand against the LORD'S anointed and be without guilt?"

Your pastor may be worse than Saul ever thought about being. He hopefully isn't trying to kill you, but he may be trying to whack you in other heartless and brutal manners. I've heard stories. But he is the pastor, the leader called by the church, and he is in authority over you. I see it this way: either respect that pastoral authority or move along. No other options. How could you, otherwise, stretch out your hand (rallying anti-pastor support from other staff members or parishioners would probably be the best example) and remain guiltless?

It doesn't mean you have to agree with everything your pastor does. I worked with my pastor, Mike Toby, for almost thirty years. Before he passed away in 2012, he would have quickly verified that I had, on rare occasions, disagreed with him on various subjects. We had argued, sometimes quite passionately, about points of disagreement – but always behind closed doors. Sometimes I was able to convince him of my side of the issue, sometimes not. Either way, he was my pastor and I chose to support his leadership and authority. He knew that when I stepped outside his office, he had my full support. I had his back, and he had mine. He gave me his support and the freedom to lead my ministry in the way I saw fit. It was mutual respect with a high level of loyalty.

As the pastor of our youth ministry, I expect the same respect and loyalty from those who work for me. When I question that from someone on our team, it changes everything. Disloyalty is a deal-breaker when it comes to team ministry. I once had a volunteer throw me under the bus while I was with a group overseas – with strong words about the work that could be done right here in Waco with all the money it took for us to go way over there. I always found myself looking over my back with him from then on. It was just a big withdrawal from the trust account.

Simply put, pastoral authority has to be a non-negotiable, or it's time to get that resumé in order.

## A Popularity Contest?

It just doesn't make sense, but it happens frequently. You hear a lot about it with insecure pastors who cannot handle great success from one of their staff members. The ego gets in the way. He wants to be the big cheese, and everyone needs to do their job – but not bigger or better than he. Back to the Saul/David conundrum – remember how the women sang that "Saul has slain his thousands and David his ten thousands"? That just ate Saul up. Didn't matter that David's success was to Israel's great benefit. What an incredibly dumb mentality! Common sense says that the more successful a staff member is the more successful the pastor is and, more importantly, the kingdom of God is increased. It all trickles up, doesn't it?

I know that I absolutely love it when those who work for me are well received. Let's face it, most of the guys and girls who work in my ministry are younger, cooler, more relevant, a lot prettier...and usually well-received and well-loved. I want them all to be ministry champions, wildly popular and even more wildly effective. That's why, as I get older, I continue to keep myself surrounded by those who could be intimidating to an aging, seemingly out of place youth pastor. They're so much cooler, and they help me so much in keeping a fresh, relevant edge to our ministry. If I was insecure about their success, I would be hurling a spear in their general direction on a regular basis.

For three years, I had Eddie James (one half of the Skit Guys) as my associate. You can easily guess that our kids loved Eddie. He was a bona fide kid magnet. And I loved it. By the way, we had some pretty good skits during those days. The more effective he was, the more effective I was. End of statement. To think any other way would be ludicrous. In fact, I can't even wrap my brain around that kind of Saul-like mentality. David, another of my associates, was really smart and disciplined, much more than me in both areas. He has his doctorate now, is a pastor, and reads a lot thicker books than I do. Mikel was beautiful, creative, a true leader – she knew how to rally the troops to get things done – the kids would have followed her anywhere. Ronny was one of those perpetually crazy, get down and mix it up, kind of guys – he reeked of relevance and could disciple young men as good as I've ever seen. Rich was too cool – hilarious and profound – and just cool. Kimberly and Sarah were my bohemian companions who saw spirituality in Christ from a profoundly artistic and expressive perspective – and were so good at helping others to do the same. Adam just made me laugh. Blake and I pushed each other to read better books. Mark and Terri were my polar opposites in keeping it all so well organized. I could go on...

These are few of my Davids. I can honestly say that I completely enjoyed all the success they had during the time they worked for me. I have no doubt that each would vouch for that fact as well. It doesn't mean I've got it all together – not true at all. But it is pretty much true in this one area. Why would I want anything other than that?

## God's Money

Every summer when I give my interns their first paycheck, I make a ceremonious presentation. I look each one straight in the eye and state with great profundity, "I want you to realize that this paycheck represents money that people gave to God." Sometimes I think it creeps them out a little, but I want to make the point that we are held to a higher level of responsibility. This is not money that people gave to Gap or Starbucks or any other place you might work and receive a paycheck (not that you should have a less than stellar work ethic in any chosen profession). It just seems different.

I remember having that self-induced thought the day I was handed my first paycheck with the church's name printed right on there. It suddenly occurred to me that this money came out of the tithes and offerings given every week by our people – money given to God, intended for His work. It was a surreal moment for me, mainly because after one week I knew it was already the best job I ever had. And they were paying me for it.

Throughout the years I've worked with the occasional fellow staff member whose work ethic is less than ideal. As they spuriously arrange papers on their desk and talk incessantly about how busy they are, I've often been known to murmur, "How does he sleep at night? Doesn't he know that the money that pays his salary is money...?" (You know the rest.)

Obviously, it is not my self-appointed responsibility to pass judgment on these who worketh not nearly as hardest as dost myself. It does seem a little lofty and borderline pharisaical. But it shouldn't change my own personal level of motivation in my work ethic. It still boils down to the fact that they pay us to do this for a living. How cool is that? Since it is money given to God, well that just raises the ante, doesn't it?

## Do You Ever Read Any Of The Books You Burn?

Back in the '80s, I had this one kid named John who was really waffling spiritually. I was doing everything I could to relate to him – looking for that niche that could give me a foothold in his life. His favorite book was *Catcher In The Rye* – which I continually discredited even though I had never actually read it. So one day, on a whim, I picked up a copy of J.D. Salinger's classic. When I was in high school, this book was considered scandalous and was banned from many libraries. So I wasn't sure what I was getting myself into. What happened had a profound impact on my already present love for books. I really enjoyed the book. In fact, I discovered a lot of interesting insight about life – stuff that I found helpful in relating to this culture. I also discovered a new outlet in my conversations with John – which continued for a long time. Even though some sense of God had ever so slowly creeped quietly back into his life while his disdain for the local church remained as intense as ever, we still had conversations over long lunches.

Why? He knew I cared about him and listened objectively to his perspective as he listened to mine. It started back when I finally read about Holden Caulfield.

At that point, I made a decision to adjust my reading habits. In the years since, I have kept a regular rotation of a Christian-based book followed by a book you can't buy at the local Christian bookstore. I rarely deviate from this pattern. I recommend it to everyone. A few years ago, I stopped underlining things in books (mainly because it always took forever to find it) and started making notations with page numbers in my journal. Since I keep a list of the books I've read during that time on the back cover of my journal, I can quickly find a quote in any book that I've noted. I find it interesting, in thumbing through my journals, how often I quote the non-Christian books. John's other favorite book was Douglas Coupland's *Generation X* – so I read that one next. It was brilliant! Since then I've read four more of Coupland's books (and quoted him several times in this book). His *Life After God* is a must read.

Ever read *Fahrenheit 451* by Ray Bradbury? It's good. The principal character is a fireman who doesn't put out fires in this futuristic society. He actually starts them by burning books. All books are outlawed and therefore to be destroyed. He is asked by a neighbor girl if he's ever read any of the books he burns. It's a good question for those who reside in the

Christian bubble. A lot of the books we "burn" today are books we probably should read. If you do all your book buying at the local Christian bookstore, you're going to miss out on some great literary opportunities. And like I said earlier, you should always read books you don't agree with. I read Rob Bell's *Love Wins*, did you?

In Aldous Huxley's *Brave New World*, John the Savage and the Controller are talking about how the new world has effectively eliminated disease, pain, self-denial, even mosquitoes – all inconveniences:

The Savage, "But I like the inconveniences."

"We don't," said the Controller. "We prefer to do things comfortably."

"But I don't want comfort. I want God. want poetry, I want real danger, I want freedom, I want goodness. I want sin."

"In fact," said [the Controller], "you're claiming the right to be unhappy."

"All right then," said the Savage defiantly, "I'm claiming the right to be unhappy."

[The Controller continued], "Not to mention the right to grow old and ugly...the right to have... cancer; the right to have too little to eat; the right to be lousy; the right to live in...apprehension; ... the right to be tortured by unspeakable pains of every kind."

There was a long silence. "I claim them all," said the Savage at last.[2]

· · ·

The synthetic, legislated, sensualized, and sedated happiness of a *Brave New World* provides tremendous insight on the present world's all-out reach for synthetic happiness. This is insight gained from venturing out into a brave new world of literature. Don't miss out.

## The Social Media Blues

It's amazing how quickly social media has marched into our lives. Facebook started in 2004 and in three short years quickly grew to 20 million users. Right now, there are 1.5 billion folks scouring the timeline on a regular basis. Are you kidding me? Back in the very beginning, it was strictly a university thing, and I jumped on the bandwagon—using my Baylor email address to access info about students who were applying for youth staff positions. But then it started widening. All of a sudden, I was getting friend requests from high school students, then young marrieds, then junior high kids, then middle age trenders, then elementary, then people even older than me (and that's pretty old). I just looked—I'm officially sitting at 2645 Facebook friends. And to quote an old friend, I don't know half of them half as well as I should like; and I like less than half of them half as well as they deserve.[3]

Anyway, the point is...Facebook, Twitter, Insta-gram, Snapchat, TikTok...so much social media inter-action going on. Much of it good. Much of it not so good. What's not good? The obvious is the time that is consumed by our kids with these various media outlets. One survey says that they are spending almost eight hours daily with TV, video games, or internet usage. Mind boggling to say the least. Since up to 90% of teens use some kind of social media, it's easy to see how this is gobbling up their time. But I think an equally big problem is the manner in which social information is dispensed and viewed by kids. In other words, they can quickly see social situations where they have been excluded. It's instantaneous evaluation of one's social standing. Pictures of kids at a table at a restaurant that have them wondering, "Why wasn't I invited?" Over and over, they have access to information that suggests to them that they don't measure up socially. These are messages that pound loneliness into their cluttered psyches. Adding insult to injury is the propensity for some kids to digitally gloat about their popular social standing— posting pics right and left, while tweeting about all their BFFs (all the while exposing their own blatant insecurity). The result is lots of "what's wrong with me" questions, while remaining hopeful that there will be comments and "likes" about their status updates.

No easy answers here. Since it's readily available

and easily accessible, I think we definitely should encourage parents to take an occasional peek at what's on their kid's wall. I'm still dumbfounded by some of the things that kids post. (Maybe they keep forgetting that their youth minister is a friend and a fellow tweeter.) But sometimes there is information that can help us better understand what's going on in the world of these teens. If you can wrap your mind around some of the social pressures that are stressing these kids out, you are going to be better equipped to help them navigate these troubled waters. Now I love technology. But not as much as you, you see. Still I love technology. And we have to continue to discover ways to use it, but not abuse it—and especially help our kids who are suffering from social media induced depression. It's out there.

## TRICKS OF THE TRADE

In closing, a few parting shots about stuff I've found helpful along the way:

**Have A Clean Seat**: For the guys, when I'm staying in one of those cabins with a bunch of boys and a community bathroom (that is destined to quickly become overwhelmingly rancid), this is an iron-clad technique. I gather all the fellows in the bathroom, and we decide as a group which stall will be the one reserved strictly for urination. If it has urinals, this is a moot point. If not, this is a necessity. One stall for #1 – all the rest designated for #2 assignment. Think about it: with teenage boys being horrible shots, this makes great sense. I'm not joking about this. I promise, you'll never not do it again.

**Respect The Janitor**: Make sure you stay on good terms with the church custodial staff. They have power. They have ears. They know stuff about the church and its goings-on that would surprise you. And they will tell you too. Treat them well and with respect, and it will return to you in favorable ways. Do otherwise, and they can make your life miserable. In my very first church, we spent an afternoon decorating for an event. Ernie the custodian came in that evening, and thinking the event had already happened, took it all down and threw it away. We just got it back out of the trash, put it back up, and never said a word to Ernie. Gotta keep those guys on your side.

**Write It Down**: If you're not journaling, you're making a huge mistake. Years ago, we decided to emphasize journaling as a major spiritual discipline in our ministry. At the time, I was a horrible journaler. But I decided that I had to lead out in this area –

especially if I was asking our kids to make a commitment to it. So I did. Years later, journaling is a constant in my life. It serves as a great reminder of where I've been spiritually. It's a great resource for talks, and a testimony to prayers answered. It's filled with observations about life and God's involvement in that life. If there is a fire in my office, the first things I will grab will be my Mickey Mantle-autographed baseball and all my journals. Trust me, if I can do it, anyone can do it. If you're struggling in this area, start with Psalm 1 and start working your way through that book. I did that – it took me four years – it was awesome. Try it. You'll be glad you did.

**Room To Room**: When you have your group staying in a hotel, four to a room, and you can't possibly have an adult sponsor in each room, here's what you do. After all the usual room checks and after you have settled into your room and are ready for everyone else to do the same, pick up the phone and call all the kids-only rooms and say, "Hey, cut it out, I mean it!" Or "You have one minute to get those lights out!" Nine times out of ten, I will get a response, "Hey, it's Bob. He said to settle down." And I can hear kids scurrying around trying to get in bed. They may be totally on to me, but it makes me feel better.

. . .

**Plead The Fifth**: I can guarantee if you join in the conversation of discord against your pastor that might be taking place among church members, you will probably become part of the collateral damage. Stay out of the discussion, put on blinders, and stay focused on your ministry. If the pastor ends up going down, you could too. I've seen this happen.

**Your Very Own PK**: Having your own children in the ministry is really cool. My daughter went through all six years with me, and I loved it. We really enjoyed the journey together. One of the really cool perks (I wasn't expecting) was the enormous amount of kids I knew from her grade at her school. I signed up for every adult-needed opportunity – riding on the bus for field trips, serving hot dogs at volleyball games, whatever. It was like an open-ended license to do campus ministry with no administrators looking over your shoulder or questioning your motives. Can't beat that.

**The Other Side Of The World**: If it is at all possible, take kids on overseas mission trips. It is one of the most challenging and fulfilling things I do now – we're talking an absolute party to be able to witness kids gaining a global perspective. It's almost like you can see the paradigm shift right before your eyes.

Kaitlyn was so reserved that she wouldn't even look at me when she talked. When she did talk it was to answer my questions in as few words as possible. Unbelievably, she decided to sign up for our Namibian mission trip. I was surprised and excited. During the trip, she came to me and said that she wanted to share her testimony at an assembly of high school students in the capital city. Again, I was surprised and excited. She did, and I got to watch her speak confidently and effectively – and I also saw her blossom spiritually, right before my eyes. Years later, we still share breakfast occasionally and invariably Namibia will come up in our conversation. And when it does, we smile a lot.

**Study! Study! Study!**: When you speak to your kids, study! Don't shortchange them by relying on your great communication skills and flying each week by the seat of your pants. They deserve the hours required to study that you might share a fresh word from the Lord – and not some ripped off outline you got online. Set aside the time required that you might step up each and every week and teach from an overflow, rather than drawing from an empty well. I find the expression "a mile wide and an inch deep" describing way too many youth communicators. It's not right. It's shameful. We must not be guilty of it. So study.

. . .

**<u>A Man By Himself Is In Bad Company</u>**: I can't imagine that you haven't seen the survey conducted by Dr. Howard Hendricks of 246 ministers who were moral failures.[4] The results were astounding. I won't go into all the details (if this is news to you, just google it). I just want to draw attention to the fact that every last one of them had one thing in common: they had no accountability partners. There was no one who looked them in the eyes, week after week, to ask them those strong questions we need to hear regularly.[5] I'm amazed how many folks I know in ministry who have failed to maintain some kind of accountability relationships. Every week Tommy, Cliff, and Mitch help me stay away from bad company. Mainly myself. Don't make that mistake. "That is something that would never happen to me" is a statement that all of the 246 offenders said repeatedly about themselves. That didn't work out like they planned. Get yourself some accountability, no matter how hard it might be.

That's enough ranting for right now. Thanks for letting me get all of that off my chest. Now let's go ahead and wrap this puppy up.

# Chapter Eleven

# I WAS SO MUCH OLDER THEN; I'M YOUNGER THAN THAT NOW

*"Some people die at 17 and put their funerals off until 77."*
Bono

I am here to testify that a half a century plus goes by really fast. A few years ago, I was working on my Mac at Common Grounds, a truly hip coffee shop just off the Baylor campus. Sipping my beverage, earpods in place, shuffling through my iTunes, surrounded by collegiate-type people, many of whom I knew – I was a picture of hipness and relevance. But then, out of the thousands of songs in my library, the Beatles' *When I'm Sixty-Four* started playing. I stopped and listened. When that song came out in 1967, I was the age of the kids I work with now. It seemed like an eternity away back then. I wondered in that moment just how old Paul McCartney was – so I googled...a Beatle in his 70s! Wow! But then the more sobering news hit me...I was only a flash away from being 64 myself! I wondered uncomfortably, "Will you still need me, will you still feed me...when I'm 64?" Man, that was quick!

I recently found a poem in my journal that I had written on the eve of turning fifty. Apparently, I was attempting to keep my sense of humor in the face of an unwelcomed birthday. I call it "So It Goes":

The other day it occurred to me
And I had this realization
I'm much older now, my youth has gone
On a permanent vacation
Too much is saggin', my memory's draggin'
And my hearing's gone to pot
There's other stuff gone wrong with me
But I suddenly forgot!

The years click by so fast. Have you ever noticed how as you get older you can't avoid the temptation to talk about time? How quickly it is passing? At the end of the school year – you just can't resist the temptation to comment about how fast the year went. When you find out someone's son or daughter is much older than you remembered, you just have to express disbelief at how quickly the time has flown.

It's like it's somewhat therapeutic to talk about it – like maybe we could find a pause button during the conversation that would slow things down.

All six verses of Bob Dylan's *My Back Pages* end with the reflective phrase, "I was so much older then, I'm younger than that now." I like that. In fact, I really feel like that in some ways. It doesn't matter that Dylan wrote this when he was in his mid-twenties.

My good young friend and former fellow staff member, Criner, makes comments about my age regularly in a playful manner. I have told him repeatedly that one of my new life goals is to live to be a really, really old guy – so old, that he also will be older. That way, I can track him down on my walker and make fun of him for being old. It's a worthy goal. When I was "older" (like Criner's present age), I was, as Dylan sang, "rollin' high...using ideas as my maps"[1] and knew it all. Now that I'm "younger", my pride has morphed into a call chiseled into granite. My "maps" are not found in flimsy ideas like those road maps you can't ever seem to fold back the right way. Ideas are great, no debate here. But ideas meshed with life experience and mountainous perspective are even better.

Now to be truthful, sometimes the older/younger lyric flips around for me. Check out this journal entry from just a couple of years ago:

"Last night I was in a funk, to say the least. I just

really felt old – which is not a good thing in youth ministry. It's okay to be old, just not feel old. Hard for me to separate my paranoia from reality. When I sense that someone looks at me like a dinosaur, who used to be a youth ministry beast, but now appears toothless and headed quickly for the tar pits, it could be totally a fabrication in my mind. Or it could be true. I know I hated the feeling of feeling old – and that's how I felt last night. Fortunately, those times are few and far between."

## Life Goes Fast And Then You Die

Coming home from a Texas Rangers baseball game, some friends and I stopped at a convenience store. I got a Mountain Dew and an ice cream bar. My friend Chad got in the car, saw me eating my ice cream and drinking my Mountain Dew, and said, "Bob, I was wondering when you walked into that store, did you turn into a 13-year old?" Obviously, doing the Dew doesn't stop the advancement of the aging process. As time cruises by at fast-forward, there is nothing you can do to stop it. And why would you? In the words of Keith Richards of Rolling Stones' fame, "The older you get, the older you want to get."

A soliloquy by Macbeth portrays life as but "a walking shadow...a poor player, that struts and frets his hour upon the stage, and then is heard no more."[2] Life is just one hour on the stage and then you make an exit. That's it. It's really quick. It's a walking shadow, cast by a candle that is on the verge of going out. "Out, out brief candle!" Macbeth acquiesces, as if he is poignantly aware of the succinctness of it all. Seems kind of depressing, doesn't it? But the book of James pictures life as a vapor, a speck on the span of the universe, a morning fog that appears for a while and then vanishes. How present, real, and tangible is a heavy ground fog; yet three hours later the sky may be clear for a thousand miles in all directions.

That's the way life is – like eating cotton candy. It really seems like a lot of candy, but it's deceiving. As soon as it hits your tongue, it disappears like donuts in a junior high boys Sunday School class. That big, beautiful, fluffy ball of potential sweetness is...snap... gone! That's life. Poets of all ages have marveled at the brevity and uncertainty of it all. They always will.

## One Day At A Time

To move into the second half of life at the speed of light and still be doing youth ministry makes it even more interesting. I have personally adopted the time-honored motto for Alcoholics Anonymous, "One day at a time." Take it one day at a time, and always keep asking myself two questions: Do I still enjoy it? And more importantly, am I still effective at it? As long as the answer to both questions is "yes," then it's another day that I get to work with kids.

"Life's been good to me so far." So states the classic rock philosopher, Joe Walsh. He goes on, "They say I'm crazy but I have a good time."[3] How could you still be working with kids? You must be crazy. How many times have I heard reasonable facsimiles of that question coming in my general direction? How much longer are you going to do this youth ministry thing? What are you going to do when you grow up? Aren't you getting a little old for this sort of youthful madness? What a great question to be asked, a supreme compliment in my opinion – not at all like a bulbous woman being asked if she's pregnant. Not at all. Dave Barry says you should never ask a woman if she's pregnant unless you can see the baby's head crowning at that very moment. But you can keep asking me what I'm gonna do when I grow up – all you want.

The worst part about being a much older youth minister is that I have to check that little 60-69 box on all surveys and questionnaires. The best part is I get to keep sucking all the marrow out of life and doing camps and mission trips and speaking to my high school students every Wednesday night and seeing kids come to Christ and be discipled....all of that and I also get those senior movie discounts.

In Kurt Vonnegut's, *Slaughterhouse-Five*, an elderly,

dying woman takes all the breath she can muster to ask her son, "How did I get so old?"[4] I like to ask myself the question, "How did I get so young?" I was so much older then, I'm younger than that now.

On Monday morning after a two-week Christmas vacation, I can't wait to get back to work. I really enjoyed the time away with family, but as I drive to the office that morning, I am truly excited to get back to it. What a gift from God, when you realize that most people probably never really discover what they want to do with their lives. After just a few weeks working with my first youth group, I finally figured it out. I went all the way through college without a clue. And then one day a passion stirred from within that was not synthetic or seemingly temporary. I finally knew for the first time what I wanted to do with my life. What a great day it is when you make that discovery. It's one of the great days in your life. Now a lifetime of years later, it's still a great day.

T. S. Eliot said it well, "I don't believe one grows older. I think that what happens early on in life is that at a certain age one stands still and stagnates."

That's an impossibility if you want to do youth ministry one day at a time for a lifetime. Stand still and stagnate and you won't last a day because you won't be effective – and you certainly won't enjoy it. A lady from our church told me that she pointed me out to a friend of hers at a basketball game, who exclaimed, "That's not how I thought Bob Johns would look at all." Now I'm not sure what she meant by that. But I would surmise that she was surprised by how old I was. Hey, when I see my reflection, what I see in the mirror doesn't really match up with what I feel in my heart. I just don't feel as old as I look. But I guess I really do look pretty ancient for a youth minister. If nothing else, thirty years of all-nighters with junior highs is going to take some physical toil. Who cares?

## I Gotta Start Flossing

One day when I was in my late 40s, I opened a letter from my annuity board. It showed a breakdown of my projected retirement benefits – stating clearly what that would look like when I reached age 62. I stopped right there and immediately proclaimed to my wife, "Did you know that in 13 years I'm going to be 62? I gotta start flossing!" We both laughed. I don't know why flossing was the first thing that came to my mind as the realization of the closeness of the senior years sprang to my attention and the twilight of life appeared on the horizon. I guess it was because that's one of those things I have been putting off my entire life. I mean, the only time I ever floss is the night before I go to get my teeth cleaned. But while I'm sitting there in the dentist chair, I always look at those posters with all that gingivitis and those corroded gums. These are the people who didn't floss. I don't want to end up as a poster child for that. So I have always intended to start flossing. I really have.

In my first forty, and counting, years of youth ministry, I didn't always floss very well. I have let time and distance takes its toil on relationships that needed to be cultivated. And I haven't been the most disciplined person in the world. But I have lived a blessed life. If I never have another fulfilling moment in my life, I couldn't complain. To do the long haul in youth ministry, you can't put off until later the carpe diem opportunities that present themselves each and every day. In so doing, there is very little desperation intruding in a life lived in that manner. Thoreau said that way too many people live lives of quiet desperation. I can honestly say that I haven't. There was no way, not even a possibility.

In a must read for everyone, *The Brothers Karamazov*, Dostoyevsky has the Grand Inquisitor profoundly say, "For the secret of human existence does not consist in living, merely, but in what one lives for. Without a firm idea of what he is to live for, man will not consent to live and will sooner destroy himself than remain on the earth, even though all around him there are loaves."[5] To have something to live for is a no-brainer.

Occasionally, as I am driving a vanload of kids on some road trip, I will look in the rearview mirror at the faces – and then have one of those otherworldly type moments. I will begin to think of all the faces I have seen in rearview mirrors throughout the years. I can almost visualize some of them from my youth ministry past: Craig, Steve, Rex, Scott, Allyson, Doug, Katie, Mindy, Jeremy, Shannon, Kylie, Holly, Kristi, Lee, John, David, Megan, Alex, the list goes on. That is one of those moments when I realize that God must really like me.

As I find myself in these more mature years, I wonder when the insanity will end. When I slipped into my 60s, I actually began experiencing the best numerical years of all my years in youth ministry. Numbers aren't everything. But it's good to know that we are still reaching kids. It doesn't make sense. It's crazy. I've been the youth pastor at my church here in Waco since 1984. As I said before, when I came way back then, some people were concerned that I might be too old to be effective. Well, what can I say? So in the meantime, I just thank God that He allows me to continue on. How the story ends is still to be determined.

How will your story end? What's age really got to do with it? It's all about calling and passion to continue pursuing that calling. The remnant of youth pastors from my generation still around are proving that to be true. If that's your calling, then don't let anything deter you from it. As a wise old character in John Steinbeck's *East of Eden* mused, "No story has power, nor will it last, unless we feel in ourselves that it is true and true for us."[6] Isn't that what really matters? What's really true, according to God's will, for you? Do you feel it? Can you sense it? God's powerful play continues on, and the verse we contribute...

# ACKNOWLEDGMENTS

To First Woodway, First Burleson, and Normandale: The three splendid churches where I have served. Each one made such a valid contribution to my life and ministry. Each one let me ply my trade, even fail occasionally, and figure out how to do ministry.

To Johnny Johnson who walked up to me one day and told me that he thought I might be good working with youth—and then asked me to be his part-time youth minister. Never saw it coming. His tremendous foresight changed my life forever. I'll always be grateful.

To Eddie James and Tommy Woodard: The Skit Guys initially pushed me to write this book. From that very first weekend I had them as high school students in a DiscipleNow group, who could have imagined the years of shared ministry.

To my lifelong ministry buddies and friends since 1979: Ken Brumley, Wayne Slay, Dennis Parnell, and Dan Carson. The conversations and laughter are such a part of the tapestry of my life—it's hard to figure out how much of that is weaved into these writings.

To my very first writing group: After reading *Bird*

*by Bird* by Anne Lamott, I helped form a writing group with a couple of former students. It was my first serious venture into putting words on paper. We would meet every week on the Baylor campus to share our drafts. It was invigorating and fired up a desire within to write a book. So, I must mention Jonathan Reynolds and Craig Cunningham who were there as I began this process. Both of these guys are accomplished writers who have published multiple books. It's like the Inklings where they're J.R.R. and C.S., and I'm the other writer that no one can ever remember his name. But that's okay. I'm just a late bloomer.

To my most excellent proofreader: Vicky Kendig did an excellent job of editing this piece of work. I couldn't believe how much stuff she found that needed fixing. And I must mention my former student and associate David Rogers, my sister Janet Wynne, and my best friend Jack Norris who were the very first ones to read the first draft and give me great encouragement, even as they pointed out the many flaws.

To my accountability group—Tommy Ross, Cliff Smith, and Mitch Thompson (or as my daughter calls us, the Brotherhood of the Traveling Pants) who have been a weekly, fixed point in my often chaotic life. Keep asking me those questions.

To Barry St. Clair and Reach Out Ministries: One eventful Super Summer week at Baylor University in

1979, Barry taught his strategy for youth ministry each morning. It was five days that changed my life. I was already in my second church, with a seminary degree, and still didn't have a real game plan for how to do this thing. I left that Friday with a blueprint that changed everything.

To all the students, staff, and volunteers throughout the years: It blows my mind when I think of the thousands with whom I have crossed paths. What a blessed life it has been. I would have liked to at least put down the names of all who have worked on my staff. I thought I could start with my very first summer interns in 1981, Steve, Craig, and Rex. It was the summer when I started discovering how to delegate and empower young ministers. It was also the summer when we went and watched *Raiders of the Lost Ark* every Thursday afternoon except the week of camp. But then I would obviously forget someone. So, you know who you are—thanks for being partners in the gospel with me throughout the many years. I've married most of you and can't believe how many have managed to stay in touch. These are relationships that I continue to treasure.

And finally, to my little family: My wife Debbie, for the love and support throughout the years and the freedom she gave me to do ministry. My daughter Hannah, for many things, including the world travels we shared and so many great illustrations. I love you both and am blessed to have you as my family.

# NOTES

## 1. ONLY A FOOL

1. Michael Bradley. *Yes, Your Teen Is Crazy!* (Gig Harbor, Washington, Harbor Press, Inc 2003)
2. Geoff Moore and the Distance. "Only A Fool" by Chuck Conner, Gary Mullett, Geof Barkley, Geoff Moore, Joel McCreight *Threads* (Forefront Records 1997)
3. Matthew 18:6—Scripture quotations are from The ESV® Bible (The Holy Bible, English Standard Version®), copyright © 2001 by Crossway, a publishing ministry of Good News Publishers. Used by permission. All rights reserved.
4. 2 Corinthians 4:1—Scripture quotations taken from the (NASB) New American Standard Bible, copyright © 1960, 1971, 1977, 1995, 2020 by The Lockman Foundation. Used by permission. All rights reserved.
5. Matthew 9:37-38—Scripture quotations taken from the (NASB) New American Standard Bible, copyright © 1960, 1971, 1977, 1995, 2020 by The Lockman Foundation. Used by permission. All rights reserved.

## 2. THE MORE THINGS CHANGE, THE MORE THEY REMAIN THE SAME

1. Larry Norman. "The Great American Novel" by Larry Norman, *Only Visiting This Planet* (Verve Records 1972)
2. David Bowie. "Changes" by Larry Norman, *Hunky Dory* (RCA Records 1971)
3. Eugene Peterson. *Five Smooth Stones for Pastoral Work* (Grand Rapids, MI, Wm. B. Eerdmans Publishing Co. 1992) p.153
4. Ecclesiastes 12:13—Scripture quotations taken from the (NASB) New American Standard Bible, copyright © 1960, 1971, 1977,

1995, 2020 by The Lockman Foundation. Used by permission. All rights reserved.

5. C.S. Lewis. *Mere Christianity* (New York, HarperCollins 1952) p.226

6. Psalm 16:1-2—All Scripture quotations taken from THE MESSAGE, copyright © 1993, 2002, 2018 by Eugene Peterson. Used by permission of NavPress, represented by Tyndale House Publishers. All rights reserved.

## 3. MY TERRIFYING LITTLE SECRET

1. 2 Corinthians 12:9—Scripture quotations taken from the (NASB) New American Standard Bible, copyright © 1960, 1971, 1977, 1995, 2020 by The Lockman Foundation. Used by permission. All rights reserved

2. Michka Assayas. *Bono In Conversation* (London, Penguin Books 2005) p.34

3. C.S. Lewis. *The Problem of Pain* (New York, HarperCollins 1940) p.96

4. Psalm 18:1-2—Scripture quotations taken from the (NASB) New American Standard Bible, copyright © 1960, 1971, 1977, 1995, 2020 by The Lockman Foundation. Used by permission. All rights reserved.

5. G.K. Chesterton. *Orthodoxy* (London, Random House 1908) p.9

## 4. I'M ONE WILD 'N CRAZY GUY

1. Steve Martin. *A Wild and Crazy Guy* (San Francisco, Warner Bros 1978)

2. William Shakespeare. *Hamlet* Act III, Scene 1

3. Matthew 6:1-4—All Scripture quotations taken from THE MESSAGE, copyright © 1993, 2002, 2018 by Eugene Peterson. Used by permission of NavPress, represented by Tyndale House Publishers. All rights reserved.

4. Thomas Merton. *Conjectures of a Guilty Bystander* (New York, Crown Publishing 1965)

5. Michka Assayas. *Bono In Conversation* (London, Penguin Books 2005) p.244

6. Annie Dillard. *Pilgrim at Tinker Creek* (New York, HarperCollins 1974)

# 5. STRENGTH BREEDS STRENGTH

1. Stephen Covey. *The Seven Habits of Highly Effective People* (New York, Free Press 1989) p.263

2. Paulo Coehlo. *The Alchemist* (New York, HarperCollins 1993) p.81

3. Jeremiah 9:23-24—Scripture quotations taken from the (NASB) New American Standard Bible, copyright © 1960, 1971, 1977, 1995, 2020 by The Lockman Foundation. Used by permission. All rights reserved.

# 6. THE ONE AND ONLY MISSION STATEMENT

1. Stephen Covey. *The Seven Habits of Highly Effective People* (New York, Free Press 1989) p.97

2. Ibid, p.97

3. Matthew 28:19-20—Scripture quotations are from The ESV® Bible (The Holy Bible, English Standard Version®), copyright © 2001 by Crossway, a publishing ministry of Good News Publishers. Used by permission. All rights reserved.

4. Doug Fields. *Purpose-Driven Youth Ministry* (Grand Rapids, MI, Zondervan 1998)

5. Thomas Merton. *Contemplative Prayer* (New York, Image Books 1969)

6. John 4:34—Scripture quotations taken from the (NASB) New American Standard Bible, copyright © 1960, 1971, 1977, 1995, 2020 by The Lockman Foundation. Used by permission. All rights reserved.

7. John 15:9-10—All Scripture quotations taken from THE MESSAGE, copyright © 1993, 2002, 2018 by Eugene Peterson. Used by permission of NavPress, represented by Tyndale House Publishers. All rights reserved.

## 7. WHAT GOES UP, MUST COME DOWN

1. Tim Hansel. *You Gotta Keep Dancin': In the Midst of Life's Hurts You Can Choose Joy* (Elgin, IL, DC Cook Publishing 1985) p.57

2. *Parenthood.* Dir. Ron Howard. Universal Pictures 1989

3. Neil Young. "Hey, Hey, My, My (Into the Black)" by Neil Young. *Rust Never Sleeps* (Reprise Records 1979)

4. Mark Buchanan, *The Holy Wild* (Grand Rapids, MI, Multnomah Publishers 2003) p.170

5. C.S. Lewis. *The Screwtape Letters* (New York, HarperCollins 1942) p.73

6. Ephesians 3:17-18— All Scripture quotations taken from THE MESSAGE, copyright © 1993, 2002, 2018 by Eugene Peterson. Used by permission of NavPress, represented by Tyndale House Publishers. All rights reserved.

7. Leonard Sweet. *Soul Tsunami* (Grand Rapids, MI, Zondervan 1999)

8. C.S. Lewis. *The Screwtape Letters* (New York, HarperCollins 1942) p.74

9. Linda Vernon, 1990 winner. The Bulwer-Lytton Fiction Contest. http://www.bulwer-lytton.com/lyttony.html

10. Psalm 12:5—Scripture quotations are from The ESV® Bible (The Holy Bible, English Standard Version®), copyright © 2001 by Crossway, a publishing ministry of Good News Publishers. Used by permission. All rights reserved.

11. Paulo Coelho. *By the River Piedra I Sat Down and Wept* (London, HarperCollins 1996)

12. Fyodor Dostoyevsky. *Crime and Punishment* (London, Penguin Books 1991)

13. Anne Lamott. *Bird By Bird: Instructions On Writing and Life* (New York, Anchor Books 1994)

14. Guy Clark. "The Cape" by Guy Clark, *Dublin Blues* (Elektra 1995)

# 8. ONCE UPON A TIME

1. Psalm 119:1-3, 24, 46, 59, 125—Scripture quotations taken from the (NASB) New American Standard Bible, copyright © 1960, 1971, 1977, 1995, 2020 by The Lockman Foundation. Used by permission. All rights reserved.
2. Eugene Peterson. *Five Smooth Stones for Pastoral Work* (Grand Rapids, MI, Wm. B. Eerdmans Publishing Co. 1992) p.90
3. John Piper. *Desiring God* (Colorado Springs, CO, Multnomah 2003) p.81
4. Malcolm Muggeridge. *Christ and the Media* (Vancouver, BC, Regent College Publishing 1977) p.25
5. William Shakespeare. *As You Like It,* Act II, Scene 7
6. Douglas Coupland. *Polaroids from the Dead* (New York, Harper-Collins 1996) p.179
7. Ibid, p.180
8. Ibid, p.179
9. Sheldon Vanauken. *A Severe Mercy* (New York, HarperCollins 1977) p.136
10. G.K. Chesterton. *Everlasting Man* (London, Hodder and Stoughton 1925) p.103
11. T.S. Eliot. "The Hollow Men" (published 1925 in *Poems: 1909-1025*)
12. Psalm 90:9,12—Scripture quotations taken from the (NASB) New American Standard Bible, copyright © 1960, 1971, 1977, 1995, 2020 by The Lockman Foundation. Used by permission. All rights reserved.
13. G.K. Chesterton. *Orthodoxy* (London, Wm Clowes and Sons 1908) p.207

# 9. THE SKY IS FALLING, THE SKY IS FALLING

1. Donald Miller. *Blue Like Jazz* (Nashville, TN, Thomas Nelson 2003) p.239
2. Larry Norman. "Right Here in America" by Larry Norman, *Street Level* (Solid Rock Records 1970)
3. G.K. Chesterton. *Orthodoxy* (London, Wm Clowes and Sons 1908) p.219

4.  C.S. Lewis. *The Problem of Pain* (New York, HarperCollins 1940) p.59
5.  Mark Driscoll. *Radical Reformission* (Grand Rapids, MI, Zondervan 2004) p.144
6.  John 12:43—Scripture quotations taken from the (NASB) New American Standard Bible, copyright © 1960, 1971, 1977, 1995, 2020 by The Lockman Foundation. Used by permission. All rights reserved.
7.  Rob Bell on Oprah Winfrey's "Super Soul Sunday" February 2015. "The church will continue to be even more irrelevant when it quotes letters from 2000 years ago as their best defense."
8.  G.K. Chesterton. *Orthodoxy* (London, Wm Clowes and Sons 1908) p.102
9.  Ibid, p.103
10. Steve Taylor. "Whatcha Gonna Do When Your Number's Up?" by Steve Taylor. *I Wanna Be A Clone* (Sparrow Records 1983)

# 10. AND SO ON AND SO FORTH...

1.  1 Samuel 26:7-9—Scripture quotations taken from the (NASB) New American Standard Bible, copyright © 1960, 1971, 1977, 1995, 2020 by The Lockman Foundation. Used by permission. All rights reserved.
2.  Aldous Huxley. *Brave New World* (London, Random House 1932) p.184
3.  J.R.R. Tolkien. *The Hobbit* (London, Allen and Unwin 1937) p.103
4.  Steve Farrar. *Finishing Strong* (Sisters, Oregon, Multnomah 1995) p.39-40
5.  Charles Swindoll. *Living Above The Level Of Mediocrity* (Nashville, Thomas Nelson 1987)

    [Adapted] Have you spent quality time daily in the Word and prayer during the past seven days? Have you had problems with immoral thoughts or actions in the past seven days? Have you allowed something ungodly into your mind through television, movies, computers, magazines, or music during the past week? Has your language reflected the image of Christ in your conversations during the past week? Have you been out of

God's will this past week due to a critical spirit (leading to gossip, etc.)? Have you spent quality time regularly with your family during the past week? Have you just lied about any of the above questions?

## 11. I WAS SO MUCH OLDER THEN; I'M YOUNGER THAN THAT NOW

1. Bob Dylan. "My Back Pages" by Bob Dylan. *Another Side of Bob Dylan* (Columbia 1964)
2. William Shakespeare. *Macbeth* Act V, Scene 5
3. Joe Walsh. "Life's Been Good" by Joe Walsh. *But Seriously, Folks...* (Asylum 1978)
4. Kurt Vonnegut. *Slaughterhouse-Five* (New York, Random House 1969)
5. Fyodor Dostoyevsky. *The Brothers Karamazov* (London, Penguin Books 1993) p.437
6. John Steinbeck. East of Eden (New York, Penguin Books 2002) p.316